On the Cover

Who is that lovely lady on the front cover of this book? Is she Lucy Ricardo or Ethel Mertz? Perhaps June Cleaver or Harriet Nelson? Donna Reed? Loretta Young? Maybe Margaret Anderson? How about Aunt Bee in her younger days?

Actually, she is none of them, yet all of them. That carefully coiffed gal, wearing make-up, a fitted dress, pearls, stockings and heels, just to watch television with her family in her own living room, is meant to be symbolic of all those beloved screen women, and others like them. She is there to remind us of a bygone era: those three decades—the 1950s through the 1970s—most of us middle aged or older Americans remember fondly, in part just because we were younger—ah, the joys of youth!

Our nostalgia for those days may also stem from missing *a more simple time*—one when we could just put our money in CDs or the stock market and watch it grow regularly without fail; one when we thought only the Kennedys or the Rockefellers needed trusts; and one when few of us imagined we would ever outlive our savings by spending $6,500 a month or more on long term care in a facility.

For the average, middle class person back in those days, it was rare to obtain specialized legal advice "merely" for our family's *planning* (as opposed to for a crisis or for a transaction). We also didn't go to an ear, nose and throat doctor for our sinuses. We went to our family general practitioner doctor! If we even *thought at all* about having a Last Will drawn up, we went to the neighborhood lawyer who handled everything from Adoptions to Zoning. We never *heard* of "estate planning and elder law attorneys," and we didn't know estate planning was necessary for <u>every</u> adult, rich or poor, whether age 18 or 80. Those days are long gone, of course. Now, whether in law or medicine, seeing a specialist instead of a generalist for some issues is not only smart, but a necessity.

Please allow the "lady in blue" on the front cover, who we will affectionately call "Ginny," to be your tour guide through our imaginary television studios, as we take you back to that bygone era—a time when families ate dinner all seated around the table together at an appointed time, without distraction by electronic gadgets, and gathered again by the television after homework was done. Ginny will help us see that times really have changed, and, where estate planning and elder law are concerned, it truly <u>is</u> necessary *these* days to obtain professional, specialized legal counseling.

Now Ginny says "Ladies, strap on your pearls and, men, don your cardigans, and let's see what we can learn from a stroll down memory lane together!"

Blooper Episodes in Estate Planning and Elder Law

Lessons From Prime Time TV

By Debbie J. Papay, J.D.
with Chris E. Steiner, J.D.

BAYER, PAPAY
& STEINER CO., LPA
Attorneys & Counselors at Law

Olive Grove Press, LLC
Maumee, Ohio

Publisher: Olive Grove Press, LLC www.OliveGrovePress.com
Cover Design: Mary Ross Creative Design
Front Cover Graphics: Woman—© Debra Hughes/Shutterstock.com
                      TV Set—© Nobilior/Dreamstime.com
Interior: Bright Gal Pointing—© RetroClipArt/Shutterstock.com
           Clapper Board—© Can Stock Photo Inc./PixelEmbargo
           Game Show Letter Board—© Mary Ross Creative Design
           The End—© Callahan/Shutterstock.com
Back Cover Photography: JLK Photography www.jlkphoto.com

Printed in the USA

The sources for all TV show general information were an author's childhood memories, interviews with others of a similar age group or older, and watching reruns and video clips. The source for all TV show specific details was *"Wikipedia®, The Free Encyclopedia,"* Wikimedia Foundation, Inc., Feb.-Sept. 2012. The authors make no attempt to copyright the specific TV show details presented herein and specifically exclude all such data from the copyright of this book. TV show plots and trivia questions are intended to be nostalgia invoking for entertainment only and are not intended to be relied upon for any other purpose. Plots are used for illustration purposes only and are completely fictional (see "A Preview of Our Coming Attractions", page 1). "Prizes" in the TV game show time segments were mentioned in nostalgic jest and are not actually offered for award.

Warning—Disclaimer—Although every precaution has been taken in the preparation of this book, the publisher and authors assume no responsibility for errors, omissions or statements made. Neither is any liability assumed for any loss or damages resulting or alleged to be resulting from the use of the information contained herein, nor warranty made express or implied. The purpose of this book is to educate in generalities and entertain. The publishing of this book should not be construed as legal or other professional advice, which should be sought only in person from a competent, appropriately licensed professional on a confidential basis.

ISBN: 978-0-9882695-0-7

Library of Congress Control Number: 2012916608

Dedication

To my beloved parents, Bill and Ginny, and
To the Aunts—Louise, Marie, Thelma, Jean, Ruth, & Vera,
Thank you for teaching a little girl to love and respect her
elders, and to treasure the stories.

~ Debbie

To Our Colleagues in:

The National Network of Estate Planning Attorneys,
www.nnepa.com,

Wealth Counsel, LLC, www.WealthCounsel.com

SunBridge, www.SunBridgeNetwork.com, and

the Purposeful Planning Institute,
www.purposefulplanninginstitute.com,

thank you, all, for affirming stories need to be told.

Most of all, to our clients at Bayer, Papay & Steiner Co., LPA,
thank you for bringing and entrusting your stories to us for
solving or preserving.

Important Announcements

Point of Order: It is sometimes confusing that both attorneys and investment advisors say that they "do estate planning." The term has different meanings in their two fields. As used in this book, the term is meant to refer solely to the *legal* aspects of estate planning by attorneys, which includes rendering legal advice and drafting legal documents, both to provide for a person's physical and financial well being during a period of illness, as well as transferring their assets and their legacy after death. As used in this book, the term "estate planning" does not refer to the building and protecting of wealth through the use of financial products and investments.

To purchase additional copies of this book: Please visit the publisher's website: **www.OliveGrovePress.com**. Quantity discounts and / or pickup in Maumee, Ohio, are both available. Shipping within United States.

Acknowledgements

Special thanks from Debbie to all those who helped inspire the creation of this book:

Brian M. Carder and Chris E. Steiner

Richard W. Bayer, Retired Attorney
Richard L. Randall, Attorney, Indianapolis, Indiana
Scott A. Williams, Attorney, Berea, Ohio
Scott Farnsworth, Attorney, Harmony, Florida
John A. Warnick, Attorney, Denver, Colorado
David J. Zumpano, CPA, Attorney, New Hartford, New York
Rick L. Law, Attorney, Aurora, Illinois
Victoria L. Collier, Attorney, Decatur, Georgia
Richard T. Taps, Attorney, Columbus, Ohio
Gregg W. Emch, Attorney, Toledo, Ohio, and
Dr. Ivan Misner, Founder and Chairman, BNI®

Extra special thanks to Holly Wilson, Melinda Musteric, and Nikki Kieffer, who inspire every single day at Bayer, Papay & Steiner Co., LPA.

Table of Contents

A Preview of Our Coming Attractions

This book is intended to help Americans of all ages, incomes, and net worths avoid making common "bloopers" in estate planning and elder law. "Bloopers" in this arena can permanently damage family relationships, waste hard-earned after-tax dollars, and cause miserable predicaments that impact mental, emotional, physical and financial health.

Our book's goal is to "educate to motivate." It is hoped that the reader will be educated about the consequences of falling into either one of two pits of legal quicksand, namely: (1) not having any estate planning in place at all, or (2) having either a bad plan, or a once good but now outdated plan. Which pit would you rather fall into? Either one is still quicksand! Hopefully the newly *educated* reader will be *motivated* to take immediate action on his own legal planning and urge not only his parents, but his adult children, to do likewise, in each case with the aid of the right professional.

The authors of "Blooper Episodes" endeavored to <u>not</u> "write like lawyers." This book was deliberately presented in plain English, with as little legalese as possible, and in short chapters, so it can be read easily by non-lawyers, and started, stopped and resumed at will. The education embedded within the chapters <u>is</u> sequential, though. Please don't skip any stories!

Who wants to read a dry, boring law book? Presuming the answer is "no one," this book's estate planning and elder law lessons are in the format of prime time television shows from the 1950s through the 1970s, for the nostalgic amusement of Baby Boomers and their parents. The show plots presented here use fictional television show characters in completely imaginary scripts that were never aired, filmed or even written. In fact, occasionally great artistic license was taken by bending the "time-space continuum" to alter what these shows could have included when they originally aired. However, the *types* of action taken here by our TV heroes (for example, Archie and Edith Bunker deeding their home over to their daughter, Gloria Stivic) were modeled after *absolutely true experiences* observed about clients during the legal careers of the authors and their professional colleagues. Many parents have lived to regret deeding their home to an adult child out of fear and misinformation, fueled by dire warnings from the ladies at bingo, or bad advice from the men at the barber shop.

Ladies and gentlemen, the stories you are about to read are true. Only the names, circumstances and combinations of facts have been changed to protect the identities of the real persons involved. This is real life disguised as fiction.

The laws on probate, estates, trusts, state income and estate tax, Medicaid, property rights, and other legal topics affecting estate planning and elder law, vary from state to state, and from year to year. Nothing in this book is intended as specific legal advice. The intent is to *educate the reader* that in legal and financial matters, unintended adverse consequences usually result when untrained persons do nothing, try to do it themselves, use non-specialists, or fail to keep a once good plan updated by a professional through the years. The intent is to motivate the reader to seek an ongoing, confidential advice relationship with a competent, reputable, specialized, and experienced attorney. The only legal advice intended by this book is that the reader should NOT try to handle his legal affairs himself based on a magazine article or a book, a friend's or neighbor's advice, or some boilerplate kit or form obtained from a store, the internet, or a TV call-in number. It's illegal to practice law without a license. So seemingly "official" sources—like CPA's, financial planners, bank employees, and TV personalities—may <u>not</u> render specific legal advice or prepare legal documents. They <u>may</u> provide the very valuable service of *spotting* potential legal issues and advising you to see a lawyer, but don't act on their "legal advice" yourself without independent legal counsel.

There used to be an old joke frequently displayed by wall signs above the service counters of hardware stores and repair shops across the country. One version might read something like this:

> ### *Our Hourly Repair Rates*
>
> $20 per hour, standard rate;
>
> $40 per hour, if you watch us work; or
>
> $80 per hour, if you started the job before us.

The point wryly but truthfully made is that it is less expensive (or painful) in the long run to let a trained person do certain jobs from the outset, than for an untrained person to attempt them himself and make it harder for the professional to later fix the mess made, assuming it is even fixable! Do-it-yourselfing or self-help in legal matters will typically only make your situation worse — often a swan dive into a legal quicksand pit!

We are not in the 1960s anymore. The legal and financial aspects of planning for your golden years, your own period of disability, and your estate distribution after your death, have become almost as technical and specialized as in the field of medicine. The reader is urged to respect the value of an attorney's juris doctorate degree, state testing, oath of office, duty of confidentiality, ongoing state licensure and disciplinary regulation, yearly continuing education and insurance coverage, and cumulative experience. You don't diagnose your own physical illness and write your own pharmacy prescriptions. So don't try to handle your legal "illnesses" yourself or let "medicine men" assist you. Please see a specialist, and don't delay, before your prognosis becomes incurable. By acting early, you can often *prevent* a legal illness instead of attempting to *treat* it. Be *smarter* than the average bear... or at least the characters you are about to read about in these prime time TV blooper episodes!

And NOW... without further ado...
let's get ON... with our SHOW!!

Part One

Those Dastardly Deeds

———•———

The Bunkers Unwittingly Give Away Dower Rights and Control

Archie and Edith Bunker's only child, Gloria, moved back home to live with them after college, bringing along her new husband, Michael Stivic. Things went along reasonably well, so Edith began to envision Gloria taking care of Edith in her old age. Edith dwelled on this a lot. She pestered Archie to deed their home over to Gloria, "so the government or the nursing home won't take it." Edith wanted to keep it *all in the family*. Archie finally gave in just to stifle her.

When Michael found out about the house deed, he got scared about being tied to Queens (and to Archie!). Michael had a heated argument with Gloria over this. After a lot of shouting, Michael stormed up the stairs, packed his blue jeans, and took off for parts unknown, "to get some space." He wasn't heard from for over a year.

The trouble is, shortly after Michael left, the furnace died and the roof started leaking. Archie, Edith and Gloria applied for an equity line of credit on the house for repair money. But they couldn't get *any* mortgage loan, because state law awards all married persons automatic dower rights in any real estate their spouse owns. That meant *Michael's* signature was necessary for the mortgage loan, merely by virtue of being married to Gloria. This was true even though his name wasn't on the deed with Gloria, and the Bunkers never intended to give <u>that</u> Meathead any ownership rights in their home!

Archie realized that the free union lawyer down at Archie's tool and die plant never told Archie about "dower" when he drafted the deed! He was a general practitioner with too heavy and varied a case load to talk to Archie about Archie's *reasons* for the deed or to ask any questions, like "why do you want to do this?' or "is your daughter married?" Archie was so angry about the fact that he had to ask the *Meathead* for permission to borrow on his own home, that he started having heart pain. As he clutched his chest, Archie wondered if they should have seen an attorney who specialized in estate planning and property ownership. But Archie was too proud to admit he made a mistake, especially one like <u>this</u> dingbat idea. "Oh, geez, Edith! Get me a Bromo, will youse, and make it snappy there!"

(All In The Family, 1971-1979)

The Jeffersons Forfeit Their Real Estate Tax Discount and Crown Son Lionel Their King

Before the furnace and roof problems occurred, Archie and Edith Bunker told their neighbors, *The Jeffersons,* about deeding their home over to Gloria. George and Louise Jefferson thought this was a great idea to save their own home from nursing home spend-down. They went to their car accident lawyer and had a deed prepared giving their house to their son, Lionel.

The Jeffersons were shocked when the next real estate tax bill arrived. They realized that they had lost the homestead discount on their real estate taxes because of the transfer. They no longer owned the home, so the discount wasn't available based on the age of the owner anymore—the owner was now, technically, Lionel, who was not eligible. The car accident lawyer never told them their real estate taxes would go up if they signed the deed!

George was furious at Archie for this crummy idea, and it ruined their budding friendship forever. Every time he even *looked* in the direction of the Bunker house, George got upset. That constant visual reminder of his blunder made George start thinking about moving to a better neighborhood, away from the Bunkers, maybe moving to the east side of New York City. In talking to a realtor, George was upset to learn he would need Lionel's signature to sell his own home, and that the money from the real estate closing would come in a check made payable to Lionel instead of George and Louise. The prospect of that kept George awake at night. His being awake kept Weezy awake, and the two argued about the whole mess they'd gotten into: the real estate taxes going up, Lionel's permission being needed to sell their home, Lionel receiving the sale money, and even a lost friendship with the Bunkers.

George and Louise began to wonder if they shouldn't have gone to an estate planning and asset protection attorney to discuss the deed instead of their car accident lawyer—maybe an attorney who was *counseling oriented*, instead of one who was *document oriented*—maybe one who would not just hand them the document they asked for without considerable two-way conversation and advice. As they lay awake in bed at night, they each wondered if estate planning is more about *peace of mind* instead of *pieces of paper*. Well, wondering didn't help much. It was too late. George felt he had been taken to the cleaners: the dry cleaners, that is.

(The Jeffersons, 1975-1985)

Florence Johnston Makes a Taxable Gift and Gets Fired

Luckily, the Jeffersons didn't have to be upset for very long about all their problems with the house deed. They finally won their lawsuit over George's car being rear-ended by a New York City bus. With the huge settlement, even Lionel was in a great mood with them. He happily agreed to sell "their" house so they could all move out of Queens up to Manhattan. They all wanted a piece of the pie.

Life was grand, and George hired a housekeeper for Weezy by the name of Florence Johnston. One day Florence eavesdropped on George and Louise reminiscing about how they had once deeded their home in Queens to Lionel. She didn't overhear the troubles that ensued, though, so that idea stuck in her mind as a good one.

Sometime later, when Florence was having creditor problems, she remembered what she had overheard. Her employers deeded their house to a family member, so she assumed it was a perfect solution to protect her meager assets. Florence strolled into a title company office downtown and had them prepare a deed of her house over to her sister. She signed the deed and paid the title company to record it with the county for her. That evening she celebrated her cleverness with her favorite drink, a Muscatel and ginger ale.

To make extra money for her creditor situation, Florence got a night job at G&Q Block, a nationwide tax return preparation service. Her supervisor reviewed Florence's recent tax returns with her as a training exercise. He went down their checklist of routine information gathering questions. This process uncovered that when Florence deeded her house to her sister, under the law, she gave a valuable taxable gift without realizing she was supposed to file an IRS Form 709 to properly report it. Florence didn't really owe any actual gift tax, but G&Q Block dismissed her anyway because she failed to file a required tax form. Now Florence had an employment record of being fired!

Poor Florence had no idea this chain of events could start just because she did what the Jeffersons did. She sure wished she had obtained some independent advice from a professional who had looked over her entire situation as her legal advisor and confidential, personal advocate. She wished she'd gone to an attorney who did estate planning on a full time basis in private practice. Oh, what a tangled web she had weaved!

(The Jeffersons, 1975-1985)

Aunt Bee Makes a Medicaid Disqualifying Gift

The night after he fired Florence from G&Q Block, her supervisor went out to dinner with his wife. Over appetizers he told his wife what had happened at work that day with Florence. In the next booth at the restaurant sat Deputy Barney Fife, who couldn't *help* but overhear what was said. Barney thought the supervisor sounded pretty official, with all his tax lingo. Barney assumed the man worked for the IRS. Barney thought he was getting a hot tip straight from the horse's mouth. What a stroke of luck! Barney always liked to be in the know and appear like an authority on any given subject.

That weekend Barney told Aunt Bee about what he overheard. He urged her to deed <u>her</u> home to her nephew, Sheriff Andy Taylor. He reasoned that Bee wanted Andy and Opie to inherit the house anyway. This way the nursing home or the government couldn't take it if she had a long, expensive illness. Barney made sure Aunt Bee took that extra step to file the IRS Form 709, so they were both pretty confident this was all according to Hoyle. Barney was as proud as a peacock to have helped out his two friends this way.

A couple years later, Aunt Bee's Parkinson's disease worsened. She had to move into Mayberry's only nursing home. Medicare only paid a part of the bill, and only for the first 100 days. After that, Aunt Bee had to private pay. At a cost of over $6,500 a month, all Bee's life savings were used up in less than a year. Andy went to the county welfare office and applied for Medicaid to pay Bee's nursing home bills. Imagine the look on Andy's face when the case worker pronounced Aunt Bee had disqualified herself from receiving state aid by making a Medicaid disqualifying gift of her home within the five year Medicaid look back period! Apparently <u>income tax</u> law and <u>Medicaid</u> law are completely separate worlds. Filing the Form 709 was just for tax compliance. That didn't have anything to do with Medicaid eligibility!

When Andy realized the big old hole Barney had dug him, he was as mad as a windmill in a tornado. Andy surely wished Aunt Bee had never listened to that Barney Fife! He was no more a lawyer than Otis, Floyd or Gomer were! Andy wished he had known what was going on at the time all this had happened. He reckoned he would have taken Bee to see an experienced estate planning lawyer to talk through <u>all</u> the possible consequences of this scheme before they acted on Barney's "hot tip"! Bee getting free legal advice from Barney sure had been "penny wise and pound foolish" for both Bee <u>and</u> Andy.

(The Andy Griffith Show, 1960-1968; Mayberry R.F.D. 1968-1971)

Florence Johnston Winds Up Homeless

Let's do some *checking in* with Florence Johnston. Things went from bad to worse for her. She wondered if she just had bad luck or no luck at all.

In the debtor-creditor proceedings against Florence in court, the gift of her house came to light. Florence was accused of having made a fraudulent conveyance. Then, since deeds are public records, Florence's bank also found out about the house transfer. The bank called her mortgage note due in full under the standard due on sale clause that is in the fine print of most mortgages. Florence needed her sister to deed the house back to her in order to avoid bank foreclosure, but her sister's *husband* refused to sign off his dower interest! Sister and her husband had a terrible fight about that late one night. Somehow the sister fell down their stairs, hit her head and died.

Florence's sister didn't have a Last Will and Testament or Living Trust yet leaving the house back to Florence. Without those, the sister's husband inherited Florence's house under state laws of intestate succession (meaning the laws that say who inherits your property if you die intestate, or die without a Last Will and Testament.) Sister's husband refinanced the house to pay off Florence's mortgage, keeping her substantial equity in the home and evicting her afterward! Florence was left homeless and mired in legal problems and attorney fees.

That title company attorney sure never warned Florence all this could happen as a result of eavesdropping her legal advice from the Jeffersons and signing a "simple" deed! His job was solving chain of title defects and accomplishing real estate transfers for the title company. It was not advising private clients on their big picture or all the possible legal and financial consequences of their actions. Florence asked for a *document*, not *advice*, and he gave her just what she asked for! Florence really regretted not seeing a different kind of lawyer, one who concentrated his law practice in estate planning and property rights for private clients. With 20/20 hindsight, Florence would have sought an attorney who explained to her the pro's and con's of what she wanted to do, and made alternate suggestions, based on his years of training and experience.

Florence began to realize that when you ask for a specific document, you are just buying mere word processing—namely toner on paper. What you *should* be asking for is what Abraham Lincoln said are an attorney's stock in trade: their time and advice. Florence realized estate planning should not be about *documents*. It should be about *plans that work!*

(*Checking In, 1981*)

The Stivics Pay Unexpected Taxes to "The Man"

Meanwhile, on his journey to find himself, Michael Stivic really missed sweet Gloria's kisses. Those were the days. Michael grew tired of being hungry in the commune. He returned to the Bunker household, made up with Gloria, and partook of Edith's home cooking and Archie's philosophical debates for many years. Everyone forgot about the deed situation, what with Gloria having baby Joey and all. Michael and Gloria eventually moved out and bought their own home. Years passed. Edith got sick and died, and later Archie passed on as well. The natural order of life played out in the Bunker household.

When Michael and Gloria sold the old Bunker home in Queens, they got a rude surprise. Since they already owned one principal residence, the Bunker home was considered investment property under law. That meant the Stivics had to pay capital gains taxes on its sale. If Archie had owned the property when he died, Gloria would have <u>inherited</u> the house at stepped up capital basis, meaning the home's current *fair market value* as of the date of Archie's death. But because the house was <u>gifted</u> to Gloria during Archie's lifetime, she received the house at *Archie's* capital basis, which was close to his original purchase price nearly 60 years before he died.

In those six decades the value of New York City real estate skyrocketed. Gloria had to pay a large portion of the sale proceeds in capital gains taxes she otherwise would not have had to pay. It really killed Michael to pay those unnecessary taxes to "The Man," and he was bitter about it for a long time. He thought it would have been better to keep that money *all in the family.* Archie's stubborn refusal to pay for professional advice had really cost them a lot more than the advice would have—by a few decimal points!

The real irony to Michael was that here was an opportunity to finally *prove* to Archie that he had made a mistake on something. But Archie had up and died and robbed Michael of the opportunity to gloat! After reflecting on this, Michael decided it really was best that Archie wasn't here to see the result of his stubbornness. Those taxes would have just slayed him!

(All In The Family, 1971-1979)

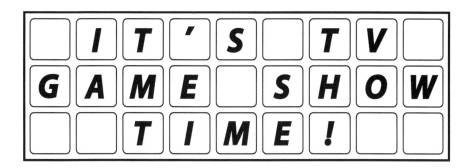

Announcer To Our Studio Audience:

Archie got his "legal advice" from Edith. The Jeffersons took theirs from Archie. Florence Johnston copied hers from the Jeffersons. Barney Fife eavesdropped some from a faceless, nameless stranger. Aunt Bee relied on Barney's expertise as an amateur lawyer. All of them caused themselves or their loved ones enormous problems and expense.

Question From Our TV Game Show Host:

For the sports car, the trip to Hawaii, and the opportunity to move on to our next round of elimination chapters, *"what was the same mistake every one of our TV heroes made?"*

Correct Answers From Our Panel of Judges:

They all tried to be "do-it-yourselfers" in a complicated professional field. They all acted on an aspect of their estate plan by self-help. They acted without counseling and advice from an attorney who concentrates in that field to see if the action was appropriate for their specific situation.

Ginny Says

*Deeding your house to another person, "to protect it", actually **doesn't** protect it, and can backfire into undesirable, unintended consequences, like these and others:*

1. You can't sell, refinance, or borrow upon the house without the new owner's permission and signature. Remember, after the deed, you are just a tenant now and the new owner is your landlord!

2. The new owner may not allow your desired changes to the home or landscaping.

3. The new owner may not insure the home the way you want it to be insured.

4. The new owner may charge you rent or evict you.

5. The IRS may impute income to the new owner in an amount equal to the fair rental value of the home.

6. The house or condo now being non-owner occupied may violate the "no rentals" clause of the subdivision or condo association restrictions.

7. The new owner could still let you live there, but refuse to give the house back to you, or give you your equity, when you need it.

8. You could be accused of avoiding your creditors (be accused of making a fraudulent conveyance).

9. You could trigger the "due on sale" clause of your mortgage.

10. You could lose your real estate tax discount.

11. The new owner loses the opportunity to inherit the house from you at stepped up capital basis.

12. You could have lost your ability to use your Internal Revenue Code Sec. 121 lifetime exclusion from capital gain on sale.

13. You could lose any voting rights connected to ownership of the home, such as in the subdivision or condo owner associations.

14. You could make yourself ineligible for Medicaid when you really need it.

15. You could be making a taxable gift over the annual exclusion amount ($14,000 per person, under year 2013 law), such that you use up some of your lifetime gifting ability and have to file a gift tax return. Depending on where you live and the value of your assets when you die, this could cost your heirs some state and/or federal estate taxes.

16. The new owner could be loyal to you, and cooperative with you, but just have circumstances happen to them beyond their control, for example: they die; they become disabled; their spouse files for divorce; they have to file bankruptcy; their creditors or predators lien or seize the ownership, etc. In each case your home is jeopardized by their legal problems.

17. The new owner's <u>spouse</u> could become an automatic co-owner if your state law awards dower. Now you are at the mercy of <u>two</u> owners.

18. In short, you completely give up control of your home and you have <u>not</u> protected it!

Ginny Says

Don't feel badly that you didn't know all this. You aren't supposed to. That's not your job. That's why they make attorneys! Attorneys don't necessarily know how to do what you do either. We all have our own purpose in life.

Don't throw the baby out with the bath water! For example, maybe there is no "dower" law in your state of residence. That doesn't mean the rest of the points about house gifting aren't valid. Actually, that difference _exactly_ illustrates the point that you need to get advice from a real live person licensed specifically in your state (not from this or any other book). That attorney will probably know <u>other</u> state-specific quirks that we did <u>not</u> include here. We have given you just a few examples.

Don't assume from reading this chapter that it is not possible to protect your home and assets. There <u>are</u> ways. These just weren't the right ones. Talk to a pro, in person. Ask your estate planning attorney about "asset protection."

Don't ever handle the legal matters affecting your assets without advice from an attorney.

_Do_ consult with an experienced attorney who _concentrates,_ not dabbles, in estate planning and administration and elder law.

_Do_ start your follow-up list or personal plan of action, right here on these lines!

Notes

_____

_____

_____

_____

_____

_____

_____

Part Two

Young Adults Are Still Adults

---•---

The Keatons Lose Parental Rights

Since the day he was born, Elyse and Steven Keaton planned for the day when they would send their son, Alex P., off to college. When he was a toddler, they just talked and dreamed. When he was in grade school, they started saving money and researching colleges and scholarships. While Alex was a high school senior, Elyse shopped store sales for the right clothes, electronics and supplies Alex would need. With all this time to prepare, Elyse was sure they had thought of everything.

Alex graduated from high school with high honors, and turned age 18 that summer. In September, Alex went off to college, fully equipped. One day in November the Keatons got a phone call from the hospital in his college town. They were told Alex had been driving home from a chess tournament when a drunk driver ran through a red light and broadsided him. Alex was in a coma. With no estate planning documents in his dorm room or glove compartment, no one there knew who had legal authority to act for Alex while he was unconscious. Elyse and Steven were shocked to learn that their parental rights over Alex had ended on his 18th birthday, the age of adulthood under law in their state. In all their preparation, they hadn't thought of <u>that</u>! They hadn't needed estate planning documents when they attended Berkeley at his age! Times must have changed in 25 years. (Imagine that.)

Without Alex having signed a <u>health care</u> power of attorney and HIPAA waiver, his parents had to go to probate <u>court</u> to be appointed legal guardian over his physical person or body. Otherwise the Keatons could not direct his medical care and get Alex moved to their own home town hospital.

Without a <u>financial</u> power of attorney in place for Alex, the Keatons also had to ask the court to be appointed legal guardian over his estate (his money and assets). Otherwise they could not legally get Alex's wrecked car out of the police impound to stop the daily storage fees and could not sign the car title over to the insurance company to receive the insurance settlement.

Elyse and Steven were flabbergasted and outraged. The mental and emotional turmoil of these realizations, and the subsequent activities they had to endure, stole their strength and attention away from helping Alex with treatment and recovery.

The court processes cost the Keatons delays, humiliation, anxiety and thousands of dollars in attorney fees, court costs, impound fees and a guardian's bond. In their minds, none of this should have even been necessary just to take care of their own flesh and blood, their own baby! Having hospitals and courts not honoring their close *family ties* was frustrating, expensive, and downright insulting.

Elyse and Steven realized they had thought of everything to prepare Alex to leave for college—everything <u>except</u> a trip to an estate planning attorney on his 18th birthday for an inexpensive "simple estate plan", including powers of attorney. The funny thing is that the Keatons had their own Wills updated just a few years ago. They wondered why their house closing lawyer didn't talk about any of this when they went back to him for Wills. It seemed like he was in such a rush and really didn't ask them very many questions about their family. They realized now that they hadn't obtained any real *legal counseling*. They wished they had gone to an estate planning attorney for competent advice and guidance about their *entire* family. An inexpensive advice session and "simple estate plan" for Alex could have prevented a lot of unnecessary suffering! The Keatons vowed they wouldn't let this happen to them again. Elyse and Steven wrote notes to themselves on their calendars flagging the 18th birthdays of Mallory, Jennifer and Andrew! Before then they would form a relationship with a lawyer who concentrated her practice in the area they needed.

(Family Ties, 1982-1989)

Fonzie's Powers of Attorney Expire With Him

Down at the police station, there was talk around the water cooler. The Alex Keaton car accident reminded the police of another accident they handled some years earlier. At that very same college had been a student named Richie Cunningham. Back in Richie's home town two hours away, four friends of his—Fonzie, Ralph, Potsie and Chachi—were sitting around Arnold's Drive-In one night. They got the idea to go visit Richie at college. The younger three wanted to meet college girls. Fonzie said he would go along just to keep them out of trouble, a fateful decision.

That Saturday Fonzie led the way to the college town on his motorcycle. The other three boys followed in one car. After they arrived at Richie's dorm and talked for a while, all five boys piled into the car to get to a party Richie heard about. On the way there, they were horsing around and not paying attention to the road. The boys were in a terrible car accident. Fonzie was killed; Richie and Potsie were severely injured; and Ralph and Chachi were miraculously thrown clear with only minor cuts and bruises.

Richie's parents came rushing to campus to be with the boys in the hospital and to make burial arrangements for Fonzie. Mr. and Mrs. "C" always had a special place in their hearts for Arthur Herbert Fonzarelli. "The Fonz," as he was known, had wisely appointed them as his attorneys-in-fact on powers of attorney (POAs) for both financial matters and health care decisions. The Cunninghams remembered to grab their copies of those legal documents as they raced out of their house.

After going to the hospital, the Cunninghams eventually wound up at the coroner's office to make arrangements and retrieve Fonzie's personal effects. They *wanted* the black leather jacket and Fronzie's favorite hair comb, but they *needed* the keys to his motorcycle, currently at risk of being towed. The coroner was not impressed with the powers of attorney Howard and Marion produced. No *thumbs up* there! He haughtily explained to them that powers of attorney expire on the death of the maker and that the documents they had were now void and useless. The coroner told them that in order to retrieve Fonzie's belongings, the Cunninghams would have to either have proof they were the Successor Trustees of Fonzie's Trust or have certified papers from a probate court appointing one of them as Executor. At this point Marion normally would have been moved to tell the coroner to "sit on it," but she had lost her usual sense of humor. All she could do was cry.

Without either kind of legal authority, the Cunninghams could not retrieve Fonzie's things. Without being able to get the motorcycle keys quickly, the treasured Triumph TR5 Trophy sat too long in the dorm parking lot and it was stolen. Without any legal tie-in to ownership of the motorcycle, the Cunninghams had problems reporting the theft to the police, getting a police report for the insurance company, and dealing with the finance company who held the title as collateral for the purchase loan. Poor Fonzie had only one more payment to go on that bike.

Running into a brick wall at every turn, Howard and Marion Cunningham decided they needed to focus on helping the living, namely their own injured son, Richie, and his best friend Potsie. As much as they loved Fonzie, all this wrangling was wasting their precious time and strength. They had a lot of problems on their hands now. These were just NOT *happy days!*

(Happy Days, 1974-1984)

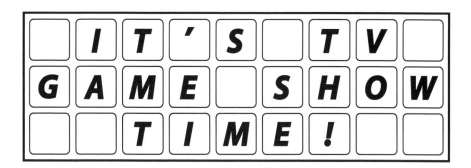

Announcer To Our Studio Audience:

Raising a child is such a gradual thing, the Keatons failed to realize Alex's 18th birthday was a huge line of demarcation, or the end of an era, from a legal standpoint. The moment Alex was no longer a minor child under their state law, Alex needed to have his own disability and estate plan in place for another person to be able to legally help him when needed.

Question From Our TV Game Show Host:

For the twelve piece patio furniture set, the trip to Europe, and the opportunity to move on to our next round of elimination chapters, *"how could the Keaton blooper episode have been avoided?"*

Correct Answers From Our Panel of Judges:

By the Keatons using an experienced attorney who concentrates in estate planning for their *own* plan, and having periodic or "five year checkups" with her, this topic would have come up when the family was discussed. Or, if the Keatons had an ongoing relationship with an estate planning attorney, instead of looking to an attorney for a one-time transaction only, they could have called her, or emailed her, and just asked "Alex is 18 now and leaving home for college. Is there anything special we should be doing?"

Ginny Says

Whatever the age of adulthood is in your state, as of that birthday every person needs at least a "simple estate plan" in place, as a bare minimum, including these planning tools:

1. **Durable Power of Attorney for Financial Affairs.** This document goes by a lot of different names (such as General Power of Attorney, Financial Power of Attorney, POA, etc.) Its purpose is to authorize someone you trust to legally handle financial matters for you if needed while you are alive but unable to handle them yourself. "Durable" means its power is still good if you become incompetent (but not after you die). These documents could take effect immediately upon signature, or could be made to have their power "spring" forth upon the happening of a certain event. Fonzie had this POA; Alex Keaton did not.

2. **Durable Power of Attorney for Health Care Decisions.** The purpose of this document is so that someone you trust can authorize medical procedures and make health care decisions for you if you are unable to do so yourself. Within this document could be a HIPAA waiver regarding the privacy of medical records, or that could be in a separate document. (Within this document could also be your wishes for your care if you are permanently unconscious, and those wishes could also be repeated in a more forceful, separate "Living Will" document.) Some states might call this POA a "health care

surrogate" document, or "health care advocate" document. Fonzie had this POA; Alex Keaton did not. Again, this POA can and should be made durable, but all powers of attorney expire on the death of the maker—the principal has no more power to delegate at that point, so neither does their agent. Your POAs expire when you do.

3. **A Simple Will.** This document gives instructions for distributing your assets after your death, chooses your Executor, grants your Executor specific powers, and, if desired, nominates a guardian for your minor children and/or waives bond for your Executor and/or the guardian. This document does nothing to help you while you are alive and disabled. It is only a death instrument. Neither Fonzie nor Alex had this legal document in effect.

These documents comprise the bare bones minimum of an estate plan. Persons educated about their options often choose tools much better than these. Stay tuned!

Do I love or care about someone 18 or over who does not know they need at least a bare bones plan in place? (List names of persons to educate.)

Notes

_____

_____

_____

_____

_____

_____

$$Part\ Three$$

No Plans, Bad Plans, Old Plans

A Bad Plan: Fonzie Had POAs, But No Will

Joanie and Chachi longed to have Fonzie's comb and black leather jacket to remember him by. It broke their hearts to think of these things so personal and symbolic of Fonzie being in a box in the coroner's office, perhaps in danger of being thrown out or stolen. In their minds' eyes they envisioned the motorcycle thief riding around on Fonzie's Triumph. The thoughts made them shudder. Instead of being able to grieve for Fonzie and start the closure process, they began to fixate on how such a miserable state of affairs could have happened.

After a few days, it became apparent there was going to be a problem with no one being legally authorized to make Fonzie's funeral decisions or access his assets to pay for one. Chachi went down to the legal clinic where Fonzie had those powers of attorney drawn up naming the Cunninghams as his attorneys-in-fact. Chachi hoped maybe they had a copy of Fonzie's Will on file there. At first he was told no one could talk to him because of attorney-client confidentiality. But then Chachi showed them the newspaper article saying Fonzie was killed, so Fonzie's file was pulled. Chachi was told, "We don't have a copy of a Will in his file. As near as we can figure out from the notes, it looks like a Will wasn't even discussed. Probably both your friend and the intake person he was assigned thought your friend was too young to need a Will. Or maybe they thought your friend had too little in assets to worry about. You should probably go down to the county probate court and see what you can do without a Will." Chachi thanked them (not knowing that was all more bad advice. Court personnel are used to dealing with attorneys, because attorneys become "officers of the court" when they are sworn in upon being first admitted to the bar. The court system is not really designed for non-lawyers to navigate alone.)

That night Chachi relayed the legal clinic conversation to Joanie, especially the part about Fonzie not "having enough assets" for a Will. "That's just ridiculous!" she cried. "We can die at any age, and the less money a person has, it seems to me, the MORE important it is that it be handled right! Rich people can afford to make mistakes. They have a margin of error. People like us can't afford to!" (That Joanie was wise beyond her years.)

The next morning Chachi and Joanie drove to their county courthouse and walked into the probate court clerk's office.

"Do you have some papers you'd like to file?" one of the employees at the counter welcomed them.

"No, we're here for some information please."

"My name is Sue. How can I help you?"

"Well our good friend died. To pay for his burial, we need the insurance money from his motorcycle being stolen. We need to take care of a lot of his arrangements and obligations, and we want his personal effects. But no one will help us or let us sign for anything."

Sue turned to her computer keyboard and asked them "What case name or number is this so I can look it up for you?"

"There is no case. We don't think anyone has done anything yet. He doesn't have any relatives."

"Well, you don't have to be related to him by blood or marriage to open a case or be appointed as Executor. Why don't you let me see the Will?"

Now Joanie and Chachi just looked at each other. They had been afraid of this. Chachi told Sue, "We don't think our friend had a Will. We couldn't find one in his cigar boxes and coffee cans of important stuff, and the clinic where he had other legal documents drawn up didn't have a Will for him in their file."

Sue asked, "Did you look in his safe deposit box?"

"We tried, but his bank wouldn't even tell us if he *had* one unless we were named on the box or one of us was the court appointed Executor," Chachi explained in exasperation. "We're just stuck in this vicious circle."

Sue explained, "Well, if your friend didn't have a Will, I can tell you this is going to be slower and a lot more expensive than if he did. Also, without a Will, no matter who your friend wanted to receive his property, state law will determine who gets it now, not him. I can't advise you on that, because it's illegal to practice law without a license. But from our standpoint here at the court, if your friend didn't have a Will, he didn't choose who he trusted to be his Executor. That means someone will have to step up and *apply* to see if the Court will approve them. That involves a criminal background check, in-state residency, and a public hearing. Lastly, if your friend didn't have a Will, he didn't waive bond for his Executor. So whoever applies will have to purchase an insurance bond in order to serve. That involves a credit check, some money, and some other requirements."

Once again Joanie and Chachi locked eyes. They knew they were "toast" now. Joanie had bad credit from her charge card problems and Chachi had a criminal record from that one mistake he made as a juvenile, before Fonzi straightened him out. Neither one of them had any money for a lawyer or for an insurance bond. It looked like they were going to have to burden Howard and Marion Cunningham with all this, at a time when they had real problems of their own.

Gee, they wished Fonzie had gone to an experienced lawyer concentrating in estate planning. She would have explained how powers of attorney only helped Fonzie while he was alive and were only half a plan. Having the <u>rest</u> of a simple Will plan in place would have been a kindness to his friends and loved ones. Fonzie would not have wanted this suffering. But Fonzie didn't go to the right person. He wound up with just half a plan. Half a plan is a bad plan.

(Happy Days, 1974-1984)

A Bad Plan: Marshall Matt Dillon's Will Has a Smoking Gun

Marshall Matt Dillon wasn't originally from Dodge City, Kansas. His family came west when he was a small child. Matt still had some shirt tail relatives back east. He really didn't care for those high fallutin' sissies who had looked down on him and his parents. He rarely thought of them or talked about them. About every ten years or so he got a letter, which he just stuffed in the box on his fireplace mantel. Those people just weren't relevant to his daily life. Matt thought they probably couldn't fight their way out of a paper bag if their lives depended on it.

Matt played his cards close to his vest when it came to his feelings. Even so, Sam, the Long Branch Saloon bartender, and Matt's sidekicks, Chester and Festus, all knew he was madly in love with Miss Kitty Russell. She hung the moon as far as Matt was concerned. He just wouldn't show it or tell anyone yet, including Miss Kitty. His secret plan was to ask for her hand when he was eligible for his Marshall's pension. Matt would hang up his badge, buy a little spread along the river, and take Miss Kitty away from having to work in a saloon. He even wrote out a Will leaving his savings to her, namely his bank box of gold coins saved through the years. If he kicked the bucket before they got hitched, Matt wanted to make sure Kitty was well provided for. Matt left the Will in the hands of Doc Adams, figuring Doc would be one of the first persons to know Matt was dead.

A few years later, Matt was killed in a gunfight while Doc was out of town. Miss Kitty and Festus tearfully cleaned out his room and found the box of letters from the family they didn't know Matt had. Figuring it was only the right thing to do, and not knowing how Matt felt about it, they sent off a letter notifying Matt's family back east of his passing. Lo and behold, one of them showed up and contested Matt's Will! Under Kansas law, as well as most other states, handwritten

Wills have to be signed in a very special, technical way. Matt didn't know that, of course, so Matt's Will was declared void after the traveling circuit judge arrived. Since Miss Kitty was not a relative of Matt's, she inherited *nothing* under the state law of intestate succession (meaning the law that says who receives your property if you die intestate, or without a valid Last Will and Testament.) The love of Matt's life received not one gold coin to keep her warm and fed in her old age. Matt's sissy cousin from back east, who Matt *had never even met*, inherited the whole shootin' match, as Matt's "next of kin" under law. That cousin caught the outbound stage just in time—the angry mob from the packed courtroom was fixin' to find a rope!

Bartender Sam just wiped down the bar and shook his head at this tragic turn of events. He had a hunch Matt's cousin would go through that gold faster than corn through a goose. He watched aging Miss Kitty working so hard and wished Matt Dillon hadn't used self-help for his Will. What kind of leader had *he* been anyway? Sam wished Matt had talked to the circuit judge about the right way to do things. What a stubborn old cuss!

(Gunsmoke, 1955-1975)

A Bad Plan: A Simple Will Leaves Some
Monkees Hanging Out on a Limb

Monkeemania was sweeping the country. In 1967, with four number one albums in one year, the Monkees sold more records than the Beatles and the Rolling Stones combined. They did this despite unjust criticism from some parts of the public and press, and having to fight stereotypes, unwritten rules, and controlling practices in the music industry. Seriously underrated, these boys were actually very smart, talented and loyal to each other.

Michael Nesmith was especially forward thinking (as evidenced by his later invention of what would become MTV). While the boys were out on a nationwide tour, he squeezed in a trip to the first lawyer he could quickly find in that night's concert town. He didn't know the lawyer did mostly divorce work— he had just gone *walking down the street* from their hotel and found a law office. The excited teen receptionist recognized him by his knit hat and got Michael right in to see her boss. A Will was drawn up, autographs and photos were obtained, and off Michael went with his Will.

When the holidays rolled around, the Monkees all had plans to go visit their loved ones. They wrapped up at the studio late on Saturday night and drew straws to see who got to take the Monkeemobile Pontiac GTO. Michael lost, so the next day, a Pleasant Valley Sunday, he went to catch the last train to Clarksville. Michael was a *daydream believer*—he thought it was much better than yoga for relaxation. He was doing just that—daydreaming about his homecoming queen—when he accidentally stepped off the platform into the path of an oncoming train.

Michael's hastily drafted Will specifically left his guitars to Peter Tork, his "music" to Micky Dolenz, and his "books" to Davy Jones. Well that was an easy division to figure out as far as the 45s, LPs, 8 track and other tapes, and the boxes of novels and *individual* sheet music. But what about the books that were bound *collections* of sheet music? They were books OF music, so which were they—"books" or "music"? Who did they go to in satisfaction of the Will bequests? To Micky, or to Davy? You might think it didn't matter that much. But Michael had *quite* an investment in his collection of books of sheet music compilations. Many were first editions, and each was autographed by a very special recording artist: Elvis Presley, Bob Dylan, Buddy Holly, Ritchie Valens, the Big Bopper, Janis Joplin, Roy Orbison, Johnny Cash, Ricky Nelson, the Beatles and the Rolling Stones, among others. Their value was inestimable in dollars, and priceless in sentiment to Davy and Micky, who both wanted them, of course, but who didn't want to fight with a best friend over a dead best friend's possessions. Worst of all, poor Peter was the Executor of the Will, appointed to decide all this, put in the middle between his remaining two best friends. Eventually the three way conflict broke up the band. Years later Peter told reporters how poorly written the Will was when applied to the reality of Michael's world. He declared "Ever since then, *I'm a believer* in getting specialized legal advice!"

(The Monkees, 1966-1968)

(Just a reminder: The foregoing story is fiction.)

A Bad Plan: No Witch's Spell Can Fix
Samantha Stephens' Simple Will

Darrin Stephens was bewitched by Samantha's beauty and charm. They married and had a little girl, Tabitha. When Tabitha was 14, they had another little girl, Serena, named after Samantha's hip cousin.

Samantha's witch mother, Endora, never liked Darrin—a mere mortal—and she loved to torment him. One day she played a prank on Darrin while he was standing on the patio tending his gas grill. Endora didn't know Samantha was walking out to him with the plate of hamburger buns just at that same moment. The spell went horribly awry, and both Samantha and Darrin were killed. Dr. Bombay came right away, but even he couldn't bring them back.

At the time of the accident, Serena was 10 and Tabitha was 24. Darrin and Samantha had "simple Wills" (also known as "sweetheart Wills", "husband and wife Wills" or "I love you Wills.") Each of their Wills left the dead spouse's property to the surviving spouse. If there was no surviving spouse, the Wills provided all property was left in equal shares to their daughters. So Uncle Arthur, the named Executor, had to liquidate the Stephens' marital assets and divide the proceeds into two equal amounts of money. No problem.

Since Tabitha was over 18, she was given her money outright. Since Serena was not an adult, legally her share had to be held in a probate court guardianship. Now there were *several* problems with *this* plan. Let's ignore the unnecessary guardianship expenses and loss of privacy and control. Let's focus on the fairness of a 50/50 disbursement to or for these two children at this time in their respective lives.

Consider the girls' age difference. The Stephens had already paid for Tabitha to go to private high school, to go to summer camp six times, to have prom dresses and shoes and hairdos, to get her first car (and the second one), to go to college, to have her wisdom teeth pulled, and to have a bridal shower and a nice wedding. They didn't keep track or run a tab as they paid for these things. They didn't charge them against some imaginary account they kept for Tabitha versus one they kept for Serena. They did what they could do out of love and parenting for whoever needed what at the time. Had they lived longer, Darrin and Samantha would have done all the same things for Serena, or more, as needed. All these expenses would have come out of their marital "pot" of combined, collective monies. Consider it the family soup pot. If Darrin and Samantha had lived into their 80s, their two daughters would have received whatever was left in the pot at the time of their deaths, in equal shares, or bowls. But timing is everything. By that point in their lives, the daughters would have been parentally provided for equally in their parents' minds according to their needs. Tabitha and Serena would have been in their 40s and 50s, or 50s and 60s. But the Stephens didn't live that long. So the *timing* of ladling out the soup was different. Since the girls were 10 and 24 *at the time the soup pot was divided*, they weren't provided for equally (their soup bowls were ladled differently.) Those very expensive 14 years of a girl's life—the ones between ages 10 and 24—didn't get scooped out of the soup pot *first* before the rest was divided between two bowls. Serena was penalized, merely by being born later! Over the years, she grew to resent her older sister and be very jealous of her. At a time when Serena needed a female friend and role model most, and perhaps Tabitha could have funneled her grief into big sister nurturing, Serena's perception of the situation as "unfair treatment" split the girls apart.

Darrin and Samantha *could* have had something better for minor children than simple Wills. If they had had *living trusts*, they could have utilized a provision called a "common trust," which would substitute for the marital "pot" they *would* have used had they lived longer. The trust could have provided that the 50/50 ladling out of the soup pot would not occur until *Serena* also reached age 24. Thus the common soup pot of the family would have gotten both girls to a certain point in their lives to which their parents would have supported them. Until then, Serena's needs, similar to those past needs of Tabitha, would be met by the *trust*. In this way Serena would not have been penalized by being younger. Some people at first ask "well, isn't that penalizing Tabitha for being older?" Most parents retract that question when they think it through. First, Tabitha has already been college educated and could be working, plus she is married. She does not have the similar "need." Second, if the Stephens were alive, she would have no right to inheritance at age 24! She would not have inherited for several more decades, if ever. Third, if Tabatha really needs some help, the kind of help she would have gone to her parents for even as an adult, the trust can advance her some inheritance and later subtract it from her 50 percent bowl of soup at the ultimate ladling. That may sound confusing, but with guidance from an estate planning attorney, it is really quite simple, and ultimately more fair than dividing the only pot of soup equally between two people, one of whom has already had dinner!

By utilizing simple Wills, Darrin and Samantha Stephens' legacy was not the one they wanted to leave. If they had used living trusts, they could have treated their daughters fairly, *"even Stephens,"* if you will. It would have been a very doable "spell" to use the common soup pot formula, or in this case perhaps the soup *cauldron recipe,* had they seen the right estate planning "wizard!" If you have children more than a year or two apart in age, and you value them obtaining at least a four year college degree, the Stephens would tell you, in retrospect, hop on your broomstick and fly to your local, qualified wizard!

(Bewitched, 1964-1972)

An Old Plan: Jeannie Displeases Major Nelson's Ghost

Speaking of the supernatural world, the genie named Jeannie fell madly in love with USAF Major Anthony Nelson. How could _he_ resist that pretty blonde face, perky personality, blinding blinks and determined desire to constantly please her master? What's not to like? She was a _dream_. Eventually, after Tony got over their species differences and quit worrying about his career, they tied the knot. A baby followed, then another. Chief of All Genies Haji wasn't happy, but a somewhat more normal life ensued for the happy couple. Colonel Bellows even quit watching for a slip up.

Unfortunately, the magic carpet ride ended when Tony was killed in a routine jet test flight. Jeannie was devastated, as was Tony's best friend, US Army Corps of Engineers Major Roger Healy. They consoled each other, and Roger helped Jeannie when a man was needed with the children or for house or car issues. Roger's wife didn't like this. She divorced Roger, taking their children with her. Now Roger spent even more time with Jeannie.

After a decade or so, Jeannie's children grew up and left home. Jeannie and Roger realized they had grown to love each other. They married. More time passed. Jeannie added Roger's name to all the savings and investment accounts she had inherited from Tony through their joint accounts. Since she and Tony had joint accounts, it seemed only natural to her to have her accounts owned jointly with Roger. She thought it made things more convenient. Jeannie didn't realize how titling her assets that way now overrode the clauses of her old simple Will. It left a third of her estate to Roger, and a third to each of her two adult children from her first marriage with Tony. But it could only affect what was in her estate, not what was in joint accounts. As time had elapsed, without re-evaluating her plan, she had unraveled it.

When Jeannie later died in an ingenious genie trap, all Jeannie's money was already in Roger's name by virtue of the joint account ownership. Her children did not have any rights to one penny of their father and mother's life savings. Ultimately, when Roger later died, <u>his</u> Will naturally left all the money to *Roger's* children by his first marriage. Tony's children received nothing. Not even three wishes. The dream turned into a nightmare.

It just makes you want to blink it all away, doesn't it? Jeannie didn't know that "second marriage couples" with children from prior marriages should use *trusts* instead of Wills! Trusts can take care of your second spouse for the rest of his or her life, and then leave what's <u>left</u> to <u>your</u> children as <u>you</u> see fit! If only Jeannie had updated that old simple Will plan through the years, some of these conversations could have come up with her estate planning attorney!

(I Dream of Jeannie, 1965-1970)

No Plan: Alice Kramden Shows Ralph Who's Boss

In a prior episode about our honeymooners, we learned that Ralph Kramden made only $62 a week as a bus driver in Brooklyn. He always had a get rich quick scheme going on the side, but they never quite panned out. So savings for the Kramdens were painfully hard to come by.

Ralph and Alice talked about going to a lawyer to have Wills drawn up. They agreed that since they didn't have children, they didn't need Wills to appoint a guardian; therefore, they'd just skip spending on attorney fees. They agreed between them that whoever was the second to die would leave half their remaining money to Ed and Trixie Norton. But since Ed worked for the New York City Sewer Department, he had a really good pension. The Kramdens didn't want to give it *all* to them. At Ralph's urging, Alice reluctantly agreed to leave the other half to the Grand Exalted Brotherhood of Racoons. Ralph envisioned the royal ceremony Ed Norton and the Racoon Lodge would put on for his funeral. His chest swelled with pride at the thought.

In one of his typical shouting rants, Ralph had a massive heart attack and keeled over dead. During her short period of grief, Alice reflected back over 20 years of fighting, insults and sarcasm. If she had heard *"Bang, zoom! Straight to the moon!"* one more time, she felt she would have lost her marbles! So unlike Jeannie the genie, who innocently or neglectfully went against her and Tony Nelson's mutual wishes, Alice decided to deliberately double cross Ralph and leave "their" (now her) money to whoever she darn well pleased. "Tell ME to 'shut up', will you, Ralph?" she asked his bus driver's hat still hanging on the coat rack by the door. "You cheapskate! You should have had a separate *trust* so I would have been provided for but I couldn't change the ultimate beneficiaries for your half of the money!"

Alice decided to trade in her old apron for silk and feathers, satin and sequins. She bought the train tickets, and she and Trixie Norton ran off to join the burlesque. When they got too old to dance for their supper, they developed a comedy routine. Right from the get-go they made lots of money, had tons of fun, got to travel, and found handsome, funny, successful men who treated them with affection and <u>respect</u>. The girls had the last laugh on their "live for today" husbands! Life was like one long honeymoon now.

(The Honeymooners, 1955-1956; The Jackie Gleason Show, 1952-1970)

No Plan: There's One Less Set of Petticoats
Hanging on the Water Tower at the Junction

On the Hooterville Cannonball railway service from Hooterville to Pixley and back, Kate Bradley, of the Shady Rest Hotel in Hooterville, occasionally sat next to Lisa Douglas. Lisa and her husband, Oliver Wendell Douglas, had purchased the Old Hany Place in Pixley and renamed it Green Acres.

The ladies chatted about various things: how to make hotcakes; Arnold Ziffel's current favorite TV show; Dog's most recent antics; and sundry gossip about Sam Drucker and Uncle Joe. Eventually Kate confided to Lisa her worries about getting old and dying with three unmarried daughters. Lisa suggested Kate talk to her lawyer husband, Oliver, about a living trust. Of course she worded it a little differently than that, as Lisa put her usual spin on the English language and facts, but Kate got the gist of it.

Kate mulled on this for a while and did some reading. She learned that if she formed a trust, she would need to retitle her assets into the name of the trust for maximum effect. One regular Friday trip to the bank, Kate mentioned to the teller that she might be changing her account soon over to a trust for her three daughters. The teller looked at her savings account of $90,000 and told her, "Oh, Mrs. Bradley, you don't need to waste money on a lawyer for a trust! I can just use your savings account to open up three equal certificates of deposit, one payable on death (POD) to Betty Jo, one POD to Bobbie Jo, and one POD to Billie Jo." Kate was reluctant, but the teller assured her that was the thing to do. "A *lot* of people do it, Mrs. Bradley! Besides, you'll help me win a luggage set in the contest the bank is running right now for the employee who sells the most CDs!" So Kate caved in. Then she forgot all about making an appointment with Oliver.

Six months later, the hot water boiler at the Shady Rest Hotel died, and the place needed some other repairs. When the three $30,000 CDs matured, Kate had to cash one in. It happened to be the one designated for Betty Jo. Shortly after that, Kate had a stroke, and the cost of her care ran through all her cash. Kate's attorney-in-fact for financial matters went in to the bank and cashed in another CD, not knowing it was earmarked for any particular daughter. Kate was terminally ill, so the family used this money to prepay for her funeral and pay off all her medical bills.

Just as the last of the second $30,000 was gone, Kate died. The third CD went straight to Billie Jo, because it was payable on death to her. Her two sisters, Betty Jo and Bobbie Jo, did not receive any money at all, because "their" CDs had been used during Kate's lifetime. When her two sisters confronted her about the unfairness of this situation, Billie Jo replied "Hey, *Mom* put my name on this CD. She must have wanted *me* to have it. I'm keeping it. You've always treated me like I'm stupid, just because I'm blonde. Well I'm not going to let you do that *this* time!"

Billie Jo used her gift to move away from Petticoat Junction. Her sisters never spoke to her again. If Kate had made that appointment with Oliver, he would have urged her to see a trust attorney. The CDs could have been owned by a *trust*, or at least have been POD to a trust, and the trust would have split things *equally* among the three daughters *after* payment of all bills. Kate would have learned that it's never a good idea to use self-help to piecemeal your assets by joint titling or beneficiary designations. Everything should flow through one master plan, so no one is accidentally disinherited like Betty Jo and Billy Jo were (and for other reasons). Oh well, *that* train already left the station! There's nothing left to do but wave goodbye.

(Petticoat Junction, 1963-1970; Green Acres, 1965-1971)

No Plan: A Trust Could Have Kept a
Dallas Oil Well Flowing

In their bitter divorce, Pam Ewing received sole custody of her daughter, Princess Ewing, and her ex-husband, Bobby Ewing was awarded visitation rights. The settlement agreement required Bobby to carry a large life insurance policy on himself for the benefit of their daughter. Pam knew that if Bobby died, child support would end, and this particular Princess was going to require lots of funding, well into her 20's. Pam and Bobby were so intent on the custody, visitation and child support terms, and Bobby seemed so young and healthy, that they didn't take the time and energy to argue over the life insurance *payout method* after consultation with estate planning attorneys.

You see it coming, don't you? Yes, Bobby died shortly after the divorce, in yet one more dramatic and suspicious turn of events on the Southfork Ranch. At that time, Princess was 12. Life insurance companies can't legally pay money out to a minor child. Pam had to hire an attorney and open a probate court case to be appointed the guardian of her daughter's estate, meaning the legal keeper of her finances. The money was placed in bank certificates of deposit. Every year Pam had to file a guardian's report asking the court to approve a new budget for the coming year and proving, with receipts and canceled checks, how every penny was spent in the prior year under the old budget.

The big secret was that Pam was almost broke. Bobby's brother, J.R. Ewing, had blackmailed her into refusing any alimony or cash settlement in the divorce. Pam was too proud to admit this to her daughter or to go to Miss Ellie or anyone else for help. She worked two jobs to make ends meet. As a point of pride, Pam tried desperately not to use the guardianship monies for things Princess needed. Pam wanted the maximum amount of money to remain intact for Princess to be able to go to the best college possible when the time came. So Pam paid for

Princess to have clothes, braces, contact lenses, a cell phone, hair highlighting, and acrylic fingernails. Of course there were riding, dance and guitar lessons, concerts and ski trips. Pam scrimped this all up herself, rather than tap that guardianship account for anything other than a monthly housing and food allowance. To do that, Pam worked long hours and denied herself things she was used to—pretty clothes, spa visits, dinners out, etc. It was hard for her, but she really wanted to be the best mother possible.

Princess went to private schools and hung around with wealthy girls. She started acting like her name. When she was a high school senior, the class trip was going to be to Europe. The cost was too much for Pam to cover. She applied to the probate court to pay this from the guardianship monies. Her motion was denied! Pam was shocked and angry. If Pam had known the court would deny *this*, she would have been applying to the court all along for money for various things it *would* have approved (like the braces and contact lenses). Pam could have saved *her* money for requests that the court rejected. From her perspective, it did not make sense to substitute the *court's* judgment on what was right for her daughter for *her* own judgment as her *mother*.

Pam really wanted Princess to have the "trip experience" and not be the only one in school not attending. So Pam took out a loan for the cost. She didn't tell her daughter this, because she didn't want Princess to feel guilty about it. Pam sure wished her divorce lawyer had made her go for a consultation with an estate planning attorney! She had learned later that the life insurance could have been made payable to a *trust* so that all this court guardianship business could have been avoided. It was slow, costly, and open to reporters and salesmen. Worst of all, *Pam* was not in *control* of her daughter's money. A total *stranger* was! She could not spend the money in what she thought were her daughter's best interests. She couldn't invest it that way either. When Pam applied to move the money out of CDs earning one percent interest into some blue chip stocks selling at an unprecedented low, the court would not allow it. Pam watched those stocks double and triple as they rebounded—without it benefitting Princess.

Pam borrowed the money. Princess went on her class trip in April to Paris, Milan, Barcelona and London. She graduated in May and turned age 18 in June. Under their state law, 18 is the age of adulthood. Now that Princess was an adult, the law required the guardianship to end. All the remaining thousands of dollars had to be disbursed directly to her, outright. Pam was looking forward to getting her loan repaid, and maybe a few house repairs done, but otherwise she dreaded Princess having this money available. Pam worried they would argue about how it should be invested. Again, she wished the insurance had paid to a trust that could dole this money out to Princess over time, in installments, instead of plunking it down on her in one big lump. The suddenness of it might give her a "Hey, I've won the lottery!" mentality. Pam wondered if the insurance money would turn out more as a *burden* than a *blessing*. No, on second thought, she told herself she was probably just being silly to worry like this.

Announcer To Our Studio Audience:

Ladies and gentlemen, we interrupt this broadcast to tell you we have a special treat for you today. As *Dallas* breaks for a commercial, you, our studio audience, may choose how this show ends, from these three alternate endings taken from real legal case files:

Alternate Ending No. 1: Princess, her new boyfriend, and their many new friends, spent the summer shopping, partying and traveling until every last dime of the money was gone. Guess Princess won't be going to college in the fall!

Alternate Ending No. 2: Princess' boyfriend convinced her to buy a fancy foreign sports car with a powerful engine.

One night they went to yet another party. They drank and danced until 4 a.m. Any mother will tell you nothing good happens after midnight. On the way home, the boyfriend wanted to test the car out—"let's see what this baby can do!" Police estimated he was going over 100 m.p.h. when he lost control and wrapped the car around a tree. Princess and her boyfriend were both killed instantly.

Alternate Ending No. 3: Princess was smart and had been a good student in high school. She got a full academic scholarship to college. Princess didn't have the desperate need of the insurance money for her education that Pam had worried about. Oh happy day! That made it easier for Pam to confess to Princess she was broke and that Pam had borrowed money for the senior class trip. Pam told Princess she was struggling to make the payments. The reaction was not quite what Pam expected. Princess really was a teenager after all, with the usual baggage that often comes with that time of passage. Add to that the fact Princess had been having some attitude problems since her windfall. Learning of this insurance for the first time after her 18th birthday brought back all her old anger about the divorce and grief at her father's death. She illogically blamed both events on Pam. Princess flatly refused to pay off the loan or give any money at all to Pam!

Princess went off to college and basically forgot about her mother. Pam had to keep working her two jobs, struggling to pay bills, and driving her now 12 year old car "a little longer." Pam was very hurt in general, and angry at Princess, as well as at herself. A deep rift formed in their relationship that never healed. The life insurance idea was a good start, but there was no plan in place to receive and distribute it. All the rest of her days Pam wondered how things could have turned out differently if this money had been handled with some common sense and specialized legal skill. Regretfully, that old phrase haunted her: *failing to plan is planning to fail.*

(Dallas, 1978-1991)

Old Plans: The Twelfth Precinct
Suffers From Barney Miller's Outdated Will Plan

Captain Barney Miller and his wife, Liz, bought a house in the mid 1970s. At that time, there was no such thing as a "survivorship deed" in their state. They had to take title to the house by a "tenants in common" deed. That means Barney owned a half interest in the house and so did Liz. The Millers used their house closing lawyer to write Wills for them, too. They each left their half interest in the house, as well as all other property, to each other. The Wills provided that if the Millers were both gone, their property should go to Sgt. Philip Fish. Since Fish had so many ailments, the Millers even provided that if Fish predeceased them, their property would go equally to Det. Stan Wojchiehowicz, Det. Ron Harris, and Det. Sgt. Arthur Dietrich. The Millers had no children, and the guys at the old "One-Two" (12th Precinct) sure were a loyal, deserving bunch. The Millers named Deputy Inspector Frank Luger as their first choice Executor, with Det. Sgt. Nick Yemana as his successor if Frank could not serve at the time.

With that many layers of backup plans, the Millers thought they were all set. They never went back to their lawyer for a periodic "Will Review." (As a cop, Barney really didn't like lawyers. He knew in his heart that they didn't *all* defend criminals, but he still couldn't help stereotyping them in his mind.) So Barney and Liz never had occasion to be told that their state had enacted a new law, just a few years after their house purchase, allowing for "survivorship deeds." Those are deeds that allow a surviving joint owner to avoid probate on the death of the other owner by merely recording an affidavit and death certificate. That process saves a lot of time and money. Not knowing this, the Millers never updated their deed to the improved version available.

Barney died first, when a mountain of paper work leaning up against the holding cell in the squad room fell over and crushed him. Dietrich commented that Barney always said "this paper work will be the death of me," and that Barney didn't know how prophetic that was! Harris wrote that down to use as an idea in his next book. Liz didn't do anything about Barney's Will after he died, because their checking and savings were joint accounts, and his retirement accounts came to her as rollovers to a surviving spouse. Since she had no trouble with access to anything, she thought nothing needed to be done. She was lulled into a false sense of security (which many estate planning attorneys call the "survivorship trap").

A few years later, Liz died in a Greenwich Village subway accident. While the Millers' affairs were being handled, the Executor, Frank Luger, discovered the house was still owned in the outdated deed fashion. This meant while everything *could have been* handled in just Liz's estate, Frank also had to open a *second* probate estate regarding Barney's death from years earlier! One half of the house was still owned by Barney's estate. Not one, but two probates? Extra time, extra expense! The Millers' dear friends down at the precinct sure wished that the Millers had had their plan updated through the years! Guess a "simple Will" isn't so simple, especially if it is outdated.

(Barney Miller, 1975-1982; Fish, 1977-1978)

No Plan: Pete and Linc Must Save Julie

All three members of the Mod Squad had been recruited to the police force by Captain Adam Greer. His offer was that by working with him, the hip trio could avoid jail time for their transgressions: rebellious Pete Cochran had stolen a car after his wealthy Beverly Hills parents kicked him out; angry Linc Hayes had participated in the Watts riots near his home; and wistful Julie Barnes had been arrested for vagrancy as a runaway. This was the late 1960s, and Captain Greer needed some authentic flower children for undercover work. His regular police force could not successfully infiltrate the counter-culture to arrest its crime lords. So "one white, one black, and one blonde," as they were called, became fuzz and got to ride around in a classic Woody station wagon. Every week they lived out a police drama with pretty much nonstop action.

The regular paycheck helped Julie get an apartment. One weekend she was repainting the ceilings with psychedelic colored peace signs when she fell and hit her head on the cast iron radiator. She was only 20 years old. Julie literally lived "paycheck to paycheck," like a lot of people have to do. She didn't own *anything* other than the meager contents of her apartment. It never occurred to her to see a lawyer about a Will. Without seeing a lawyer about a Will, she didn't have occasion to talk to one about powers of attorney (POAs).

Julie's severe head injury put her into a coma. The doctors said Julie was partially paralyzed. It was obvious that if she survived, Julie was going to be institutionalized for quite a while. Julie had no blood relatives who could be found. Pete and Linc had come to regard Julie and each other as family, though. The three were "solid." The boys were absolutely distraught over this accident and wanted to help Julie. They came to see her every day. When they left, they squeezed her hand and whispered into her ear, *"Keep the faith, baby."*

After thirty days of not going to work, Julie's health insurance lapsed. The boys tried to get Medicaid to start paying Julie's current hospital and future rehab bills, but it was discovered that Julie really *did* own something after all—something everyone forgets because we don't see it on a day to day basis. Julie had a 401K plan at work with $1,600 in it. Unfortunately, as a single person having over $1,500 in assets, that 401K made Julie ineligible for Medicaid under the law—by $100. Without Julie having POAs in place, no one could spend down this 401K for Julie. Pete had to humiliate himself and go ask his parents for money for attorney fees and court costs. Linc contributed to the cause by taking off a lot of time from work to go to court and try to be appointed legal guardian over Julie. When the bond company found his arrest record, though, Linc realized he would not succeed. Captain Greer had to step in, and he was appointed instead. Being appointed guardian allowed the Captain to legally access Julie's 401K account and spend it down below $1,500 on her behalf so she could receive Medicaid. Her boss and friends would not have had to do all this if proper, up to date POAs had been in place. Julie, Julie, Julie! NOT groovy, girl!

(The Mod Squad, 1968-1973)

Bad Plans: One Father Knows Best; The Rest Don't

The day before the regular monthly meeting of the F.B.I., its Program Chairman got a cancellation call from their scheduled speaker. (Oh, this is not the F.B.I. *you* might be thinking of—although most of the meeting attendees *would* be in business suits, crisply pressed white shirts, neckties, freshly shined shoes and trim haircuts. They just would not be wearing sunglasses, badges, guns or ear pieces! No, *this* is the television studio backstage chapter of "<u>F</u>athers <u>B</u>eing <u>I</u>nvolved," a group of breadwinning, concerned fathers who take their family responsibilities *very* seriously.)

The Program Chairman was in a panic for a speaker. On this short notice, he could not find anyone. He knew he'd have to cover the allotted time himself. He racked his brain for something that might be of interest to the members. Then he remembered he had recently been to an estate planning seminar and heard the importance of having powers of attorney (POAs) for financial matters in place. He raced to an office supply store and bought a pack of form POAs. That night when the members gathered, he took the podium and relayed, second hand, what he had heard at the estate planning seminar, or at least as well as he could remember. He handed out blank form POAs to all the fathers. The members all filled their forms out within the week, and that was the end of it. They all had the false sense of security that this matter was "handled," so none of them went to an estate planning attorney for further consultation on their *entire* plan for themselves *and* their families.

Over the next several years, many of the fathers encountered circumstances where it was desirable that their attorney-in-fact named in the POA be able to <u>use </u>the POA to help the father or his family. The circumstances varied—illness, accident, being away on a business trip or vacation, being detained unexpectedly at the studio, incarceration, rehabilitation, kidnapping and held hostage, lost in the wilderness, you name it. As the circumstances unfolded, each father, or his poor wife or children, discovered the folly of using self-help to obtain and complete legal "forms."

Dr. Alex Stone (Donna's husband), had his signature notarized on the POA, but he didn't also have two witnesses sign it. For the purpose for which it was needed, under his state law, that was necessary. No one would honor Alex' POA at crunch time.

Lucas McCain had one witness sign his POA, because one just happened to be there at the time and that felt "official." But there was no second witness hanging around, and he had never heard of a "notary" out West in the 1880's. His POA was no good exactly when it was needed most. Boy did he want to set his *rifleman's* sights on that Program Chairman!

Amos McCoy had Luke and Little Luke sign as witnesses on his POA. Both signatures were "no good" because Little Luke was a minor and Luke was the person appointed in the document. That POA sure wasn't the real McCoy!

Ricky Ricardo guessed his POA had to be notarized, so he took it into the bank with him. The notary was so flustered by his good looks and Cuban accent, she forgot to put her notarial seal under her signature, printed name, and commission expiration date. When Lucy went to use his POA, *no bananas*!

Dr. John Robinson was in a stressful time when he got the form POA. He and his wife, Dr. Maureen Robinson, and their children, Judy, Penny and Will, were in the running to be chosen as an astronaut family. If chosen, they might get to travel in the Jupiter 2 to a planet circling Alpha Centauri. He was so distracted. You might say his mind was *lost in space*. He started filling out the form, noticed that it might need to be notarized, and stopped. John later found a notary and signed the document in his presence. The family *was* selected for the mission. While they were gone, John's brother needed to use the POA on his behalf. The financial institution would not accept it, though, because the date above John's signature was one day (the day he started the form), and the date above the notary's signature was another day. *"Oh, the pain… the pain."*

Rob Petrie's wife, Laura, needed to use his POA to sign a paper having to do with their real estate, meaning their house. It was signed, witnessed and notarized, but the witnesses didn't print their names under their signatures and their signatures were illegible. Also one witness signed using a red pen—it just happened to be what she had in her hand at the time. Each of these reasons alone was enough for the county recorder to refuse to accept the document for recording under their particular rules. *Rob had been tripped up by more than his own ottoman!*

Ward Cleaver's POA was signed correctly for his state of residence. The only trouble is that by the time June needed to use it, it was over ten years old. *Jeepers, Ward!* The institution would not accept a POA that old. Ward never thought to go see an estate planning lawyer at least once a decade, or more often, to tune up his plan and keep it current.

Danny Williams' POA was also signed correctly, except the person he appointed as his attorney-in-fact in the document was his first wife, Margaret. After she died, and he married Kathy, he was so busy between the tour, the kids, and his new wife, he didn't think to go to an estate planning lawyer and get a new POA. Daddy just didn't *make room* in his schedule for that.

Ozzie Nelson's POA was signed correctly for his state of residence. But when his son, David, tried to use it after Harriet died, David found out that the POA wasn't a very good one. Being a boilerplate form from a store, it wasn't artfully written and didn't cover certain counseling issues. For example, David needed to gift Ozzie's money to himself and Ricky in order to do some further legal work for Medicaid planning. The POA didn't specifically allow gifts to the appointed attorney-in-fact, so an institution refused to honor it on the objection that David was self-dealing. Even if they had ignored that elephant in the room, the POA didn't specifically authorize gifts over the annual federal exclusion amount (which then was $10,000 per person, per year—nowhere near enough to handle Ozzie Nelson's situation!)

A man named Brady and his lovely lady were in a car accident. Carol was killed and Michael was badly injured, looking at a recovery and therapy period of a year or more. Their housekeeper and trusted friend, Alice, was the backup attorney-in-fact named in Michael's POA to serve after Carol. Alice wanted to use the POA to create a trust to take care of Michael and the six kids. But the POA did not contain the power to create a trust. The Brady Bunch was in a bunch of trouble.

Steve Douglas and his three sons had trouble with the quality of the POA wording as well. When Steve was out of the country at an aeronautical engineer's symposium, the family dog, Tramp, became very ill. Uncle Charley wanted to use the POA to put the dog to sleep. The veterinarian said the POA didn't contain any clauses like that, and he was fearful that Steve would read him the riot act when he came home. A delay ensued that was stressful for everyone.

The form POA had a blank line to insert the signer's social security number on it, presumably for identification purposes. Andy Griffith dutifully filled his in when he signed the POA. Andy had filled out enough police reports in his day to know you just don't leave a line empty! By the time it came time to use the POA, identity theft had become a phenomenon, as did public access to government records. The POA needed to be recorded down at the county recorder's office so it could be used regarding real estate. Andy's Mayberry friends in the recorder's office didn't want Andy to have his social security number on a public document showing up on a public website. Yet the social security number couldn't be blacked out on the POA, because that was an alteration to the document, which meant the county recorder would not accept it. This was just a bad form document. There was no reason to include his social security number in a POA!

Out of the whole crew, only Jim Anderson had second thoughts about using a boiler plate form. He thought "how can this document be any good?" Jim went to an office supply store to read the box in which the forms were sold. Right there on the package was this warning:

> This product is intended for information use only and is not a substitute for legal advice. State laws vary and change and the information or forms do not necessarily conform to the laws or requirements of your state. While you always have the right to prepare your own documents and act as your own attorney, do consult an attorney on all legal matters. This product was not necessarily prepared by a person licensed to practice law in your state.

Jim went home and told Margaret what he had read. They decided not to use the free form. The next day they scheduled an appointment with an estate planning attorney who was highly recommended to them. They obtained an estate plan to provide for themselves *and* their children during any period of disability, and to pass on their assets and a bit of their legacy after their deaths. The Andersons met with their attorney for counseling and to review everything every few years. When illness and death struck, as they always will, the Andersons had a common sense and effective plan in place so they could focus on the important things in life. In short, their plan was successful. *Guess Father Anderson really DOES know best!*

(The F.B.I., 1965-1974; The Donna Reed Show, 1958-1966; The Rifleman, 1958-1963; The Real McCoys, 1957-1963; I Love Lucy, 1951-1957; Lost in Space, 1965-1968; The Dick Van Dyke Show, 1961-1966; Leave It To Beaver, 1957-1963; Make Room for Daddy, 1953-1964; Adventures of Ozzie & Harriet, 1952-1966; The Brady Bunch, 1969-1974; My Three Sons, 1960-1972; The Andy Griffith Show, 1960-1968; Father Knows Best, 1954-1960)

(All stories are fiction in regard to the names used.)

An Old Plan: The First National Bank of Partridge

Shirley Partridge lived alone in her condo now. Her children, Keith, Laurie, Danny, Chris and Tracy, had all grown up and moved on to lives of their own.

One night Shirley was making herself some Jiffy Pop on the stove top. She didn't really like popcorn that much, but she loved to watch the flat tin foil unfold into a globe. The tin reminded her of the old TV dinners they had occasionally back in the day. But what Shirley really loved was the way those tightly packed tin swirls unfolded so perfectly. She needed some order in her life. Her thoughts were chaotic. That day at lunch the band's long time manager, Reuben Kincaid, put down his fork and said "Shirley, *I think I love you.*" Shirley laughed and told him, "Well when you know for sure, tell me then." Reuben responded, "I'm serious. Why don't we get married?"

Shirley got a Coca-Cola out of the ice box as she wondered what she should do. Reuben was nice and understood her. He was smart, gentle and funny. They had been friends for years and knew each other's histories. There should be no surprises. It would be helpful to have someone to share life's troubles with, and she sure was lonely at night. The marriage seemed logical. She told herself, *"C'mon, get happy* about it." But something was holding her back from joy.

Shirley thought about how Reuben had five kids of his own. There were still royalties and other income rolling in to her from the eight Partridge Family albums and related merchandise. If, make that <u>when</u> Shirley died, she didn't want the fruit of their labors to go to <u>ten</u> children. Any future income that stemmed from all those years of hard work and riding around in a school bus should go strictly to <u>her</u> children. She knew a prenuptial agreement was needed before she married Reuben. Shirley decided to call her music industry lawyer in the morning to get referred to the right attorney specialist.

As she moved to the couch with her popcorn and Coke, Shirley started thinking about what this prenuptial agreement should say. That led her to thinking about what would be fair to Reuben, as her husband, from a financial perspective, if Shirley died first. Then she mulled what would be fair to her and his children, respectively, if Reuben died first. Shirley thought the prenup's purpose was to provide for the possibility of *divorce* and a dispute over assets brought into the marriage and acquired since then. That didn't solve the problems of the marriage ending by *death*. *Then* how would the money be handled? It was at that point Shirley remembered that her Will was about 20 years old. She thought about how it directed where her money would go, namely "to my children in equal shares."

As Shirley thought about THAT, she really got upset and even more confused. *Is equal always fair? Does fair always have to be equal?* Right now an equal five way split didn't seem very fair to her at all. Through the years, Shirley had handed her adult children money so many times, she felt like the FNBP—the "First National Bank of Partridge" as she called herself. In fact, she had a little notebook labeled "FNBP" that she went and retrieved from her desk. When Laurie needed a divorce attorney and a move to an apartment, Shirley handed Laurie a check for $25,000. When Keith needed all new crowns on his teeth, she laid out $30,000. Danny had totaled his car in an accident. It was old, so he didn't get much insurance money. But that left him with no transportation for music gigs. So Shirley provided $45,000 for a van with custom made storage for music instruments. Chris constantly needed money to help with various things for himself and his own children. And Tracy… well, Tracy had never asked for anything! Bless her heart.

The reason Shirley kept her little FNBP notebook was that she wanted to keep track of these financial transactions until she figured out what to do about them. At the time she wrote out each check, she had it in her mind that these amounts should be "advancements" against future inheritance—meaning the five shares should be evened up after she died by considering what inheritance each child had been advanced while she was alive. But the collective tab was growing so big, she wondered if there would be enough money to even it up! What if her final illness ate up most of her money? What if Tracy got nowhere near what the others had already received by begging? That didn't seem "fair"!

Shirley never told the kids she meant the checks as advancements. She wanted to see how they treated them. Each time she handed over the check, each child muttered something along the lines of "Thanks, Mom. You're a lifesaver. I'll pay you back." Laurie did pay back a little, but then she became ill and lost her job. The payments stopped and nothing more was said. But Danny, that darn Danny! He wound up making regular payments for a long time and paid back every red cent, plus interest! She was so proud of him. Gee, Shirley suddenly realized she should write "repaid in full" in her FNBP book by Danny's name and amount. If the kids found the book, they might think Danny should still be treated as having received a $45,000 advancement. (Why hadn't Shirley kept a record of payments?) In fact, she was sure there would be some arguing after she was gone. Sibling rivalry would erupt out of grief. "Mom always liked you best" would be uttered. The size of some loans would be a surprise to the others. Some kids would claim their money was a gift, not an advancement; some would claim they repaid in full when they didn't. Fingers would be pointed. What a mess.

All this angst still left unanswered Shirley's earlier question of *"is equal always fair?"* Shouldn't Danny get a little something extra for being the only one who lived up to his promise of repayment? And maybe Tracy should, too, for never having asked. Laurie was starting to develop some serious health issues affecting her employability. If the other four children were well set financially, couldn't she receive a little more than the others and that still be "fair?"

Gifts, loans, advancements. Repayment, no repayment. Interest, no interest. Children with special needs, children without. Shirley was starting to get a headache. Shirley looked at her little dog, Simone III, patiently waiting for popcorn to fall on the floor. "Don't worry, girl. I'll call tomorrow for an appointment with an estate planning specialist. I can't be the first parent with this problem. There must be a mechanism to handle loans, or whatever they were. I'll get that 20 year old Will replaced. Let's not think about it anymore tonight, or we'll go crazy. We'll think about that in the next episode."

Announcer To Our Studio Audience:

Little did Shirley know, these gifts/loans/advancements could also be a Medicaid problem and an estate or gift tax issue! It's a good thing Shirley is going for professional help!

(The Partridge Family, 1970-1974)

A Bad Plan: Richard Kimble's One-Armed Man Enriches the State of Indiana

Dr. Richard Kimble owned life insurance on his own life, payable to his wife, Helen, as beneficiary. Helen owned life insurance on her own life, payable to her husband, Richard, as beneficiary. The Kimbles had no children.

After Helen died and Richard was arrested and charged with her murder, the life insurance company froze her policy. Once Richard was convicted of murdering his wife, the insurance company determined it would not pay out to him, per its standard fine print about murderous beneficiaries.

Richard escaped from police custody in a train derailment accident while en route to death row. After that he was on the lamb for several years in search of the real killer, the one-armed man. In hot pursuit of Richard was the determined police Lieutenant Philip Gerard. Richard was just a *little* busy with searching for the killer, hiding out, and finding temp jobs. So nothing transpired on his appeal in court, Helen's probate estate, or the search for her heirs other than Richard. The life insurance company could not let the claim be in limbo forever. After a few years, it paid the money into the State of Indiana Unclaimed Property Division.

Eventually Richard found the one-armed man. Richard's conviction was overturned and he was freed. But by then his life was in shambles. He had no medical career left. The Kimble home had been foreclosed on in the years Richard was running and not making payments. His credit was shot. His delayed grief over the loss of Helen let loose. Richard took to drowning his sorrows in alcohol. One winter night, under its evil influence, Richard passed out in an alley and later died of exposure.

Richard's Will had been lost in the process of the house being emptied in the foreclosure eviction. All the Kimble possessions were just put out on the curb. One of Richard's doctor friends applied to the probate court to open Richard's estate without a Will. The good doctor made application for the life insurance on Richard's life. The policy's beneficiary was Helen, but she was deceased. So the insurance company paid the money to Richard's probate estate. With no Will and no known next of kin, this money also went to the State of Indiana, this time not as unclaimed funds, but under the law of escheat. You see when you don't have a Will, or a workable Will, your home state has one for you. It is called the law of intestate succession, and it dictates where your money goes if you haven't successfully provided for that. The law sets forth the priorities by which various next of kin inherit. It provides that in cases of no next of kin, your money escheats, or transfers "to the crown," or nowadays to your state government.

The really sad part is that Richard and Helen had some charities that were very near and dear to their hearts. Since Richard was a pediatrician, they gave money annually to The Smile Train, a children's charity providing cleft lip and palate repair. They had several other charities on their "A" list as well. Richard and Helen would have wanted their insurance proceeds to go to those charities. When you think about it, the one-armed man not only killed Helen and destroyed Richard's life, but ultimately caused two huge life insurance policies to be paid to the State of Indiana. Enrichment of the crown might have been avoided if the Kimbles had living trusts. The life insurance policies could have been owned and/or payable to living trusts. The trusts would have had backup trustees to replace the Kimbles, and those trustees could have made claims. The trusts could have also had charities as backup beneficiaries. Living trusts are very common planning tools to sensibly handle life insurance policies and provide for multiple contingencies with much more detail than a beneficiary card can hold!

(*The Fugitive*, 1963-1967)

A Bad Plan: The Ingalls Accidentally Disinherit
Their Loved Ones on the Prairie

To say that Charles and Carolyn Ingalls loved children is an understatement. They had Mary, Laura, Carrie, and Grace together. A son, Charles, Jr., died as an infant. They adopted Albert, Cassandra and James, who they loved just the same as their blood children. When Mary married Adam Kendall and Laura married Almanzo Wilder, they loved them like sons. Ask anyone who knew the Ingalls—Mr. Edwards, the Olesons, Doc Baker, Lars Hanson—they'd say Charles and Carolyn had a broad definition of what "family" means. Reverend Alden would tell you the Ingalls had "bottomless hearts."

After many years of challenges in the 1870s and 1880s in Walnut Grove, Minnesota, the Ingalls moved again, away from their little house on the prairie. This time their luck improved. While Charles was digging a well, he discovered their land held mammoth veins of copper and silver. Soon they had more money than you could shake a stick at. Years passed. The Ingalls' seven children started having children of their own. Charles and Carolyn reveled in the joys of grandparenthood without any worries about money.

Albert married a widow woman with two toddlers. They moved to be near Charles and Carolyn, who grew especially fond of this daughter-in-law and those babies. When Albert died young of a blood disorder, the Ingalls asked Albert's wife and children to move in with them. The entire household grew to regard each other with love as "family." The Ingalls looked upon Albert's stepchildren no differently than their blood grandchildren. Their hearts did not make distinctions. In fact, since the children lived with them and they saw them daily, those two grandchildren were the Ingalls' favorites, if truth be told. Ultimately, Albert's widow and her children took care of the Ingalls in their respective final illnesses.

All this made the conclusion of the show especially tragic. You see Charles and Carolyn had "simple Wills." The wording left all their property, including their copper and silver riches, "in equal shares to our issue, per stirpes." The lawyer they used for their Wills focused mainly on mining rights and contracts having to do with land. He just used a Will format he found in one of his law books and never counseled the Ingalls as to whether they wanted their property to trickle down their family tree "per stirpes" or "per capita." He also never asked them how they felt about in-laws or step-grandchildren. By the way those Wills were worded, without special attention to the details as applied to the Ingalls family, Albert's children did not inherit Albert's equal one-seventh share. The reason is that they were Albert's *step*children, not his issue by blood, nor brought into the fold by legal adoption. Nor did their mother, the Ingalls' caregiver, inherit her husband's one-seventh, because in-laws were not included in the wording of the Wills. That is certainly not what Charles and Carolyn would have wanted! Once again we see "simple Wills" are not so simple and should not be treated that way, either by the person wanting an estate plan, or the person providing it!

(Little House On The Prairie, 1974-1983)

A Bad Plan: Kotter Would Welcome Back His Sweathogs

Gabe Kotter arrived home after a long day of teaching at James Buchanan High in Brooklyn. He found his wife, Julie, reading the mail just inside the door of their apartment. She looked very pale and shaken. "Did I ever tell you about my Uncle Randolph?" she asked him. She went on to explain that he was very rich, and childless. Apparently Julie was his favorite niece. The letter was from a lawyer, informing Julie she had just inherited quite a bit of money. Gabe and Julie read the letter several times and talked about it all night. The money wasn't enough to retire, but it was a good chunk! They brainstormed what would be the best use of it. While Gabe loved teaching and seeing the difference he made in the lives of his Sweathogs, he was burned out with Vice Principal Woodman, the school board, the union, and the parents. Julie had a college degree in anthropology, but ultimately became a hairdresser. She was tired of the long hours on her feet, and her knees, hips and back were killing her. The Kotters decided they should use the inheritance to quit being employees and become bosses. They could buy themselves a job to last them until retirement. They could say "up your nose with a rubber hose" to their employers and have a great life. No more of Julie's tuna casserole!

So the Kotters found a business broker and bought two franchises, plunking down most of their cash. Gabe chose a Fastprint Print Shop. Julie chose a Two Hour Photo Store. They used the rest of the inheritance to buy equipment and lease space. They quit their jobs and opened up shop, expecting customers to pour in and their employees to do all the work while they "supervised." It didn't happen quite like that. The Kotters soon realized they had absolutely no training or experience in marketing, managing, accounting, payroll, governmental compliance, or other business skills, let alone in printing or photo developing. Their lack of preparation as business owners coincided with the timing of changing technology trends. Many small printers and photo developers nationwide were made obsolete by affordable home and office laser printers and high quality, high speed photocopiers becoming available, as well as the big box stores entering into inexpensive photo developing. After a painful seven year run, the Kotters closed both businesses and were left deeply in debt.

Gabe felt as if he were Vinnie Barbarino asking "What? Where? Why?" What had happened to them? Now the Kotters were in a real bind. Julie could get her hairdresser's license back without great difficulty, but she had lost her client base. She'd have to start from scratch. Her aching joints were now seven years older. Gabe's teaching license had expired. He felt too old, broke and tired to return to college to renew it. If he did get his license, the school district would have to pay him at a pay grade that considered his prior years of experience, so he'd be competing against less expensive new hires coming right out of college. With this gap in his resume, Gabe wondered if he could even get a teaching job. Kotter would not necessarily be welcomed back.

Gabe and Julie realized that receiving that inheritance in a lump sum enabled them to make bad decisions. They were able to buy their franchises with cash instead of applying for bank purchase loans. The banks would have required detailed business plans. Preparing the plans would have made the Kotters realize they were acting rashly and didn't have necessary know-how. The inheritance from Julie's uncle, meant as a blessing, wound up being a curse. The Kotters lost not only Julie's inheritance, but all their own savings, and now they had no careers to fall back on. If only that uncle had left the money in a trust for them. It could have been invested for their retirement, or doled out to them annually like an extra income stream or private annuity. The uncle's plan was just "nutsy cuckoo," as Vice Principal Woodman would say. Uncle Rudolph should have had some more specialized advice.

(Welcome Back, Kotter, 1975-1979)

A Bad Plan: Legal Self-Help Proves a Mission Impossible

Jim Phelps, of the IMF (Impossible Missions Force), knew that come Monday there would be a self-destructing tape recording with instructions for him. Then he'd be off on another covert mission against evil. These trips seemed to get more dangerous each time. Through the years he had read news reports of the long term unconscious—Karen Quinlan, Nancy Cruzan and Terri Schiavo, among others. Jim remembered the news reporters repeatedly said that "everyone needs a living will." So that weekend Jim went online and found himself a living will, printed it out, filled in the blanks and signed it.

Jim must have been acting on a premonition, because he was indeed injured on his next mission. While he was unconscious in the hospital, the doctors needed someone to authorize a dangerous surgery for Jim. They needed to discuss Jim's condition with someone for whom he had waived HIPAA privacy protections. The living will was produced. Unfortunately, Jim had listened to reporters, instead of an attorney concentrating in estate planning. The living will did Jim no good. What Jim needed to have in place instead was a health care power of attorney. *Everyone* does not need a living will, because not everyone may agree with what their state prescribed living will format says. But what everyone *does* need is a health care power of attorney with appropriate HIPAA clauses. This would allow a trusted person to speak with the doctors, ascertain a medical condition, and authorize procedures. Guess your mission really was impossible, Jim, if you relied on reporters for your legal advice!

(Mission Impossible, 1966-1973)

Announcer To Our Studio Audience:

HIPAA is the acronym for a federal law entitled "The Health Insurance Portability and Accountability Act of 1996." This law covers many types of issues related to health care. The part most relevant to our estate planning discussion is the Privacy Rule, which had an effective compliance date of April 14, 2003. This rule regulates the use and disclosure of protected health information. The law is very complex and contains stiff monetary penalties for violations. Doctors and other health care workers are understandably very guarded about disclosing medical information to family members or friends of a patient who do not have written HIPAA authorization from the patient. This can interfere with the patient receiving prompt treatment.

(Editor's Note: To fully appreciate how this law can interfere with one's daily life, we offer this true story. A co-author's 80 year old father was in a nursing home from fall, 2002, until his passing in May, 2003. On April 14, 2003, the co-author made one of her regular between-visit phone calls to the nursing home from a distance of an hour and a half away. She asked, "How's my dad doing today? Did he eat his breakfast?" The nursing home worker responded with "I'm sorry, HIPAA started. We can't talk to you anymore." You can imagine what was said after that! Our point to you is this: estate planning attorneys don't live in books and computers. They live in the real world. They not only know of their multiple clients' experiences, they have parents, siblings, spouses, and children. Often they have been in the hospital themselves. They know firsthand that the most stressful time in your life will be when you or someone you love is seriously ill or dying. Why would you want to wait and have to deal with lawyers and legal matters at those crunch times? It is so much less stressful to get everything done while you and your family members are well and the prospect of using your or their estate plan seems remote. You've heard that expression that in your final months or years, you will *never* say "Gee, I wish I had spent more time at the office instead of with my family." Similarly, you'll *never* say "Gee, I'm glad I had to pile on a couple trips to the lawyer under the gun when my mom was sick instead of spending quality time with her (or managing my own job and family)." Make your life easier by planning ahead and doing so properly—not on the advice of a layman or news reporter, but with that of a professional.)

An Old Plan: Michael Brady Unblends His Blended Family With a Bunch of Woes

Here's the story of a man named Brady. Michael still had an old Will from before the time when his three sons were born. His first wife and he were always talking about revising their husband and wife Wills. The holdup was that they could never agree on who to name as guardian for Greg, Peter and Bobby. So nothing got done before Mike's wife died. Then Mike was suddenly overwhelmed with being both a dad <u>and</u> a mom, and an architect. Just as he got all that under control, Mike's energies turned to being a new husband to his bride, Carol, and new father to her three girls with hair of gold, Marcia, Jan and Cindy. (At this point we should explain to you that Carol is still alive and the Brady car accident in our earlier "Fathers Being Involved" chapter was just a dream—like the finale of *Newhart* or the entire ninth season of *Dallas*.)

As Christmas rolled around one year for the Bradys, Mike had a full day of shopping planned. Carol gave him a long list of gifts to find for the six kids: Ouija, Twister, Barbie, Rock 'em Sock 'em Robots, Hands Down, Chatty Cathy, Etch-a-Sketch, G.I. Joe, Easy Bake Oven, The Game of Life, Barrel of Monkeys, Operation, Battleship, Walkie Talkies, Lite-Brite, Thingmaker, Mouse Trap, model racing cars, an ant farm, Troll dolls, and of course the usual replenishment of worn out, lost or broken hula hoops, Play-Doh, Legos, Sea Monkeys and Super Balls. As it got later in the day and his list was still long, Mike started to hurry on icy December roads. He was killed in a car accident.

Michael's old Will was of little value, since it left everything to his now deceased first wife with no alternate plan. Since the Will was outdated and incomplete, the fallback position took over: Mike's state of legal residence had a Will for him under the law created by its legislators. That law, called the law of intestate succession, contained formulas for dividing up a decedent's assets in cases where there was an insufficient

Will. The law provided that Mike's wife, Carol, who was not the natural or adoptive mother of his three sons, would only receive $20,000 and a third of Mike's estate. Carol's daughters, who Mike loved dearly, received no parental support from Mike. His sons were to inherit the other two-thirds of his estate. Since Mike's sons were minors, their inheritance had to go into a guardianship until they became legal adults. Mike's estate consisted of the family home, all his savings and investments, and a life insurance policy provided by his employer. Now Carol had to be a mother to six children (after <u>applying</u> to the court to be appointed guardian of the boys), but somehow support herself and her three daughters. The boys' needs were well provided for from the guardianship fund, while the girls were "poor." This blended family didn't blend very well. Oh, Mike! Why didn't you keep your plan up to date with the events of your life and provide for <u>all</u> your loved ones?

(The Brady Bunch, 1969-1974)

Old Plans: Gilligan's Friends Wish They Could Vote Themselves Off the Island

Seven stranded castaways sat around a fire one night on their uncharted Pacific isle. Their three-hour tour had run into a tropical storm that grounded and wrecked their charter boat, the S.S. Minnow. They'd been here for three months now. They were beginning to accept they'd be here for a long, long time, with no phones, no lights, and no motor cars. They had not a single luxury.

Mary Ann broke the silence by remarking, "You know, just like *that* your world can be turned topsy-turvy. You can leave home that morning thinking you'll be back soon, but then not return. I'm worried sick about what happened to my dog I left in a kennel in Kansas before I left for Hawaii. I wish I had implemented one of those pet trusts I read about."

Ginger responded with "Well, I'm worried about not signing my movie contract. I wish I had left a power of attorney with my sister to do that for me. It doesn't start filming for two years, so I just know we'll be home by then. But since I didn't sign it, I'm worried they'll give the part to someone else. Why didn't I do that?"

Thurston Howell, III, offered that he hoped he and Lovey were home by then as well. Thurston was worried the boards of directors for his various endeavors would have him declared dead if he didn't show up by the statutory deadline. He had been talking about having a trust with a successor trustee to manage his property, and thus the voting rights to his stock, but he just hadn't signed it yet. He was sorry he procrastinated.

The Professor was just as anxious. Earlier that day he learned from the Radio Announcer that his home state had re-enacted its state estate tax since the time the group was shipwrecked. Professor Roy remembered that if life insurance is payable to your estate, like his was, his state would include it in his taxable estate. He muttered aloud, "Well, I've got to get back and change the beneficiary on my life insurance from my estate to a trust, or it is going to get estate taxed."

Life insurance! The mention of that sure broke the reverie. "Oh, no!" Gilligan cried. "My life insurance is still payable to my ex-wife. I need to change that right away! I'd rather Skinny Mulligan get it than her!"

As he looked at his Little Buddy, the Skipper remembered how he first met Gilligan. Although his First Mate seemed a lot younger (probably because of his naïve demeanor), the gap was only 14 years. They both served in the Navy's Seventh Fleet in World War II. They met when Gilligan pushed the Skipper out of the way of a loose depth charge. After that, they became fast friends. Thinking about WW II and now hearing this conversation about life insurance, Skipper remembered with a jolt that he still had some VA life insurance payable to his mother! She had been dead some time. He wondered what would happen to that money if he died before he could change that beneficiary designation. He'd rather see his Little Buddy get it if possible than have it be unclaimed.

The Skipper made a general comment out loud about wanting to change his VA life insurance. That made everyone think about their life insurance. Several of the castaways realized they had a lot of small straggling policies from various sources. Some were purchased and some were provided to them for one reason or another: AAA, AARP, Sears, J.C. Penney, their credit unions, and employer policies. They couldn't even remember who they had scribbled in on some of the beneficiary cards!

Just then the castaways were all startled as their frequent companion, the Radio Announcer, spoke out. He made a public service announcement encouraging everyone to conduct annual reviews with their financial planners and estate planning attorneys to go over their assets and legal plans. Now just HOW did that guy always seem to know what was happening on their tropic isle, but not ever send them a rescue party?

(*Gilligan's Island, 1964-1967*)

Bad Plans: You'd Think the Second Generation Would Get Smart

Agent 86, or Maxwell Smart, as some called him, and Agent 99, were secret agents for CONTROL, a secret government counter-intelligence agency. After months of working together, surviving numerous plots by KAOS agents through Smart's dumb luck and 99's skills, the two fell in love. Their personal lives became intertwined. After Agent 99's mother died, 99 shared with 86 how she had to pay over $22,000 in state estate taxes. That didn't sound right to Smart, because 99's parents did not appear to be wealthy. So the two ace agents set off to investigate this. They learned that the estate tax exemption for her parents' state of residence was $340,000 per person. *Would you believe*...Agent 99's parents had $680,000 in assets at the time her mother died? The trouble stemmed from the fact that 99's parents had simple Wills instead of tax trusts. That meant that when 99's father died with only a Will, he naively threw away his tax "coupon" or exemption. When 99's mother subsequently died, her parents as a couple had only one exemption left, so the amount of assets in excess of that exemption was taxed. If Agent 99's parents had basic married-couple tax trusts instead of Wills, they could have used two exemptions instead of one. The state estate tax Agent 99 would have had to pay would have been <u>zero</u> instead of $22,000. It was as if her parents went to the grocery store with a $20 coupon and left it in the car. *"The Old Save a Few Dollars in Legal Fees by Getting Simple Wills Instead of Trusts Trick"* cost Agent 99 over $22,000 in taxes! Now you would think this caper would have taught Agent 99 the value of getting specialized estate planning advice. Hold onto that thought as our episode unfolds.

Max eventually proposed marriage to Agent 99. The two were wed and went off on a long honeymoon. *Sorry about that, Chief.* A few months after they returned, Agent 99 called Max on his shoe phone while he was driving. She told him that she had not been feeling well lately. Max said *"Don't tell me you're pregnant!"* half jokingly. "Why, yes I am!" she replied.

"99, I ASKED you not to tell me that!" But Max was very pleased and told his bride that he couldn't wait to get home to talk about it. His dumb luck didn't save him that day, however. As he was putting his shoe back on while driving, Max lost control of the car on a curve and drove off the cliff. *He missed it by THAT much.*

Fang consoled 99 as best he could. Several months later she delivered twins, a boy and a girl. After that the years flew by. In 99's retirement, her son told her that his wife was going to divorce him. Not wanting her son to lose any inheritance from her in a divorce, 99 asked her daughter for help. Agent 99 suggested she would leave everything to her daughter in her Will in case her son's divorce wasn't final yet, with the understanding that the daughter should give half to her twin brother when the coast was clear for him to receive money. The daughter agreed, in what was to become *"The Old Say You Will But Then You Don't Trick."* Agent 99's daughter was mad at her brother over how (she thought) he neglected their mother during her final illness. *Would you believe…*she didn't ante up half like she promised when the time came to do so? Agent 99 had explained her plan to her son, so he knew the intent. He brought a lawsuit against his twin sister to recover "his half." The bitter battle split them apart forever. If only Agent 99 had learned her lesson during her parents' estate administration. If she had seen an estate planning lawyer, her son's half could have been placed in an asset protection trust for him. With some decent planning, her twins would not have become enemies for life. Agent 99 *missed a good plan by THAT much!*

(Get Smart, 1965-1970)

A Bad Plan: Fred Sanford Really Does Have the Big One, Elizabeth

Fred G. Sanford had been getting forgetful lately. Grady and Bubba had to constantly prod him when they were playing cards. Fred thought maybe the problem was this new pill he was taking for his arthur-itis. He was even more blunt than usual, too, constantly insulting Ethel. She would just tell him to "WATCH IT, sucka!" and swing her purse at him.

One day Fred's fiancé, Donna Harris, took Fred to her attorney to have Fred draw up a new Will. The marriage plans were moving along slowly, and she wanted to button things up before too much more time passed. Fred's prior Will left everything to his son, Lamont. The new Will left Fred's estate half to Lamont, and half to Donna, his intended wife. When they got back to the house from the attorney's office, nothing was said to Lamont about the change.

About a month later, Lamont and Fred were having an argument. Fred called Lamont a big dummy, and Lamont called Fred an old fool. Suddenly Fred clutched his chest and gasped "It's the big one! You hear that, Elizabeth?" he asked rolling his eyes heavenward. "I'm coming to join ya, honey!" Lamont just looked at him, thinking Fred was pulling his usual routine. Unfortunately, this time Fred was not crying wolf, and he died on the floor while Lamont stared at him skeptically.

At the funeral home, Fred's doctor approached Lamont and offered his condolences. The doctor suggested Fred's quick passing may have been a blessing compared to the Alzheimer's he was facing. Lamont was stunned. Fred had not told him he had been diagnosed with that illness! When Lamont later found out about the Will change after the date of Fred's diagnosis, Lamont brought a lawsuit to have the new Will declared invalid. In the lawsuit, Lamont accused Donna of exerting undue influence on Fred while he was mentally incompetent. After thinking through how much this lawsuit would cost and what little there was to fight over, Donna and

Lamont agreed to a settlement. Lamont would get the house and the bank accounts; Donna would get all the personal property inside the house. Lamont had always wanted to move out of the Watts section of Los Angeles anyway. He thought this would be a good way to get Donna to clean out the house for him before he listed it for sale. He thought he had outwitted Donna.

Well, Donna had the last laugh on Lamont! As she moved furniture out, Donna noticed one corner of carpeting was raised up a little. She pulled it and found thin, flat plastic bags of $100 bills underneath. Then hidden up on the basement rafters and under the basement stairs she found Chock Full of Nuts cans full of money. Donna knew that folks who remember the Great Depression always have a stash somewhere. Her best find, though, was up in the attic. There in their original wrappings without a single dog-eared corner or wrinkle in them were unopened packs of baseball cards from 1910. The appraisals came in at nearly $3 million for these valuable collector's items! Can't you just hear Fred speaking from the grave: "Lamont, you big dummy! Why didn't you watch my health better and get me in to see an estate planning lawyer for a trust that would own all my property and of which *you'd* be Trustee?"

(*Sanford & Son, 1971-1977*)

A Bad Plan: Sergeant Joe Friday Books the Beneficiaries

Two very serious men walked up to the receptionist at a posh L.A. law firm. The first one said to her "My name's Friday. This is Officer Frank Smith. We're here about the homicide." The distraught receptionist immediately showed them into the Managing Partner's office. In answer to their questions, the partner told Friday and Smith the background regarding one of their lawyers who was found slain in the building's underground parking garage. It seems a very wealthy woman, Mrs. Penobscot, came to the firm for an estate plan ten years ago. She was assigned to the murdered lawyer, John Justdoit, who was a newbie back then. John drafted a Will for his new client, leaving her estate in equal shares, outright, to her nine adult children, and appointing himself as her Executor. A year ago Mrs. Penobscot died. That's where this tale starts. *The story you are about to read is true. Only the names have been changed to protect the senseless.*

After Mrs. Penobscot died, John Justdoit probated her Will, charging a hefty but standard attorney's fee (waiving the Executor's fee), plus reimbursement of all his expenses, totaling about five percent of her estate. After paying state and federal estate taxes, inheritance taxes, income taxes, probate court costs, and appraisal fees, the considerably reduced estate was distributed outright by large checks payable to Mrs. Penobscot's nine children in equal shares. Those nine children did not fare well with their sudden lump sum windfalls. None of them had any experience handling money. They had always had money doled out to them. Now, overnight, that management stopped.

Andrew Penobscot had an alcohol dependency. His check enabled him to no longer need his job. Instead of drinking only at night, he lived in a perpetual state of inebriation. Everything in his life became neglected and ruined. His family left him and he was constantly ill with alcohol related ailments.

Bruce Penobscot had a drug addiction. His windfall enabled him to quit rationing himself on the quantity or potency of the drugs he could afford. Bruce died in an accidental overdose.

Charlotte Penobscot had a shopping problem. Her money was soon gone, spent on first class world travel to shop in fashion meccas.

Deidre Penobscot was comparatively stable as far as this family goes. However, her husband had his own ideas how to use the inheritance check. He decided now was the time to join an expensive country club, buy a sailboat (which he promptly sank, uninsured) and then a small plane (that he crashed, killing himself and all their children). Fortunately Deidre was not on the flight, but the loss of her entire family caused her to have a mental illness and a downward spiral.

Edward Penobscot had a weakness for gambling. His inheritance check enabled him to pay off his gambling debts and now bet even larger amounts on more risky wagers. He quickly got in over his head, welched on some large losses, and ended up feeding the fishes with cement shoes.

Franklin Penobscot had a sex addiction. We'll say no more about that to our PG rated audience other than that he wound up beaten, robbed, destitute and with several serious diseases.

Grace Penobscot had always enjoyed magazines showing photos of well decorated homes with very elaborate landscaping. She spent every dime of her bequest on purchasing, redecorating and re-landscaping a mansion in Beverly Hills. Then she had no money left for the house cleaning help or gardeners to maintain the situation, nor the very high real estate taxes and utilities, nor the furniture, painting and window treatment loans or mortgage loan payments. Foreclosure was commenced against her. The Sheriff's sale in a down real estate market brought in less than she owed. Grace wound up with no home and multiple court judgments against her. She had been better off in her less expensive but affordable home.

Henrietta Penobscot already had quite a bit of debt when her mother died. Her charge card bills and other creditors took most of her inheritance, and she quickly spent the rest in her giddiness at being released from those problems. She was right back to square one.

Isabella Penobscot was the baby of the family. She was young, beautiful, sexy, and happy. That girl loved to party! Predators took all her money. The parties were over. Food and rent are the party girl's issues now.

As they gathered for the funeral visitation time for Bruce, the remaining seven brothers and sisters talked. They figured out that the entire Penobscot fortune was gone and they were in worse condition than before they inherited their windfalls. A busybody from the funeral in the adjoining visitation room overhead most of this. She came over and explained how some of these problems could have been avoided by use of a living trust that doled the inheritance out over time instead of dumping it on the siblings in one lump sum. The children decided to adjourn to a nearby cocktail lounge, where they remained all night. By dawn their alcohol and rage induced plot was hatched. The Penobscots went to their mother's law firm building and hid by the elevator in the underground parking garage. When John Justdoit got out of his red Mercedes convertible, they circled him like wolves and beat him to death. They had planned this—everyone hit and kicked him so they would never know which one person killed him—sort of like a firing squad principle. Then they fled, with no witnesses… except the security camera on the wall that caught the whole grisly scene. Friday and Smith rounded up all the perps and charged them with murder and conspiracy to commit murder, among other crimes. The Penobscot siblings all received death sentences and were taken to prison.

Now you, gentle member of our studio audience, may say this tale is all too outrageous to be true, contrary to our claim at the outset that all our stories are based on true legal files, or compilations of them. We would reply that it is all...can you guess?...wait for it...wait...it is all...*just the facts, ma'am!* (Oh, come ON now, you KNEW that was coming, didn't you?)

(Dragnet 1951-1959; 1967-1970)

Announcer to Our Studio Audience:

The co-authors want to promptly confess. While the *ways* that the nine Penobscot heirs blew their sudden inheritance are all typical events compiled from various true cases, we really do not know of any lawyer beaten to death by disgruntled heirs. Artistic license was taken in order to create the need for a *Dragnet* homicide investigation.

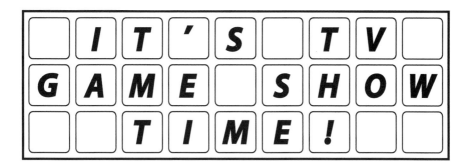

Announcer To Our Studio Audience:

By now our studio audience has already learned the morals of this book. So we won't quiz you on those anymore! Instead we will provide you some light amusement to refresh your brain for the next section. Please listen carefully.

Question From Our TV Game Show Host:

For the Vespa Scooter, the trip to Disneyland, and the opportunity to move on to our next round of elimination chapters, *can you name the 1950s-1970s TV shows in which each of the following items was prominently or regularly featured?* (The answers follow by corresponding question number.)

1. Beautifully decorated antique bottle with stopper

2. Champagne bubbles floating in the air

3. Modified Winchester Model 1892 Rifle

4. Phasers, photon torpedoes, and communicators

5. Rebus puzzle

6. Hourglass with sand running through it

7. Enamelware coffeepot sitting on a wood stove at the end of the show

8. Beulah the Buzzer

9. Zonk

10. Swinging fence section that spanks a corny comedian

11. Armless living hand residing in a box

12. View of a portly silhouette stepping into a caricature

13. A ranch map, branded, then going up in flames

14. Shoe phone, and a cone of silence

15. Three sets of vintage ladies underwear hanging over the edge of a railroad water tower

16. A loudly ticking timepiece

17. A speaker phone used to meet with the boss

18. The S.S. Minnow

19. Self destructing tape recordings

20. A management office in a fenced cage area

21. A script letter "L" embroidered on a shirt or sweater

22. Doghouse and tree trunk tunnel entrances, coffeepot listening device, rising bunk beds, endless disguises, barbed wire, mud, Carter's lab, and LeBeau's strudel

23. A rumpled raincoat worn over a suit and tie

24. Men's hair comb

25. Nuclear submarine and the Flying Sub

26. A Pepsi and milk

27. Wire rimmed glasses, knit khaki hat, and clipboard

28. Red telephone, fireman's pole, cave garage

29. Prosthetic arm

30. Telephone high up on a telephone pole

31. 1960-1964 Chevrolet Corvettes and Sting Rays

32. The Striped Tomato, 1974-76 Red Ford Gran Torino

33. Story-telling paintings in a creepy art gallery

34. _____ (remember your own!)

35. _____

36. _____

37. _____

38. _____

Correct Answers From Our Panel of Judges:

1. I Dream of Jeannie

2. The Lawrence Welk Show

3. The Rifleman

4. Star Trek

5. Concentration

6. Days Of Our Lives

7. Gunsmoke

8. Truth or Consequences

9. Let's Make a Deal

10. Hee Haw

11. The Addams Family

12. Alfred Hitchcock Presents

13. Bonanza

14. Get Smart

15. Petticoat Junction

16. 60 Minutes

17. Charlie's Angels

18. Gilligan's Island

19. Mission Impossible

20. Taxi

21. Laverne & Shirley

22. Hogan's Heroes

23. Columbo

24. Happy Days (Fonzie) or 77 Sunset Strip (Kookie)

25. Voyage to the Bottom of the Sea

26. Laverne & Shirley

27. M*A*S*H (Corporal Walter Eugene "Radar" O'Reilly)

28. Batman

29. The Fugitive

30. Green Acres

31. Route 66

32. Starsky and Hutch

33. Night Gallery

34. _____

35. _____

36. _____

37. _____

38. _____

If you'd like a "mulligan", or a chance to replace any wrong answer you may have had above, then correctly answer the following question: *for what name or title is "M*A*S*H" an abbreviation?* You can check your answer in the next "It's TV Game Show Time!" segment, at Correct Answer number 25.

Ginny Says

Wow! You just read 21 fact-based plots illustrating probably double that number in self-inflicted legal problems. This reminds me of another of my favorite TV show characters, a colorful Robin, who might say something like this about those blooper episodes:

"HOLY String of Bad Decisions, Batman! Why did these poor victims fight the forces of evil alone? Why didn't they have Commissioner Gordon shine the Bat-Signal into the Gotham night sky to get help from a pro? On second thought, I guess that would be too complicated for John Q. Public. But there *was* an easy alternative—instead of going it alone, they could have just met with an attorney specializing in estate planning!"

Enough said? Are you ready to move on to the stories of people who did it the RIGHT way? You don't even have to get up from the couch to go put more tin foil on the rabbit ears or turn the channel dial. For our next thrilling episode, just turn the page!

Part Four

Good Plans!

Good Plans: Mary Richards Turns Her Smile on the World of Trusts

As Associate Producer of the Six O'Clock News at TV station WJM in Minneapolis, Mary Richards routinely reviewed newspapers from around the country, especially the Midwest. One day an Ohio newspaper caught her eye. An article explained that reporters had reviewed an estimated 2,000 county probate court case files from the prior year. The article went on to reveal the names of a list of people, their ages, dates of death, occupations, and how much money was in their estates. ("County Gains From Thrift of Departed," *The Blade,* Toledo, Ohio, March, 1997.) Mary mentally noted that most court files are public records open to everyone, so all this kind of data is readily available if you looked for it. Mary wondered if her TV station should do a news segment on this topic. She thought about pitching the idea to Lou Grant. But she could just hear Murray Slaughter and Ted Baxter complaining about how much research would be involved, so she didn't pursue it. Before Mary moved on to other news articles, her last thought on this one was "Gee, I know it is public information if you go look it up, but how would I feel if I saw my parents' names and personal data printed in a newspaper for all the world to see?"

Four years later Mary happened upon another Ohio newspaper article. This time the topic was four-term Ohio governor James Rhodes. The article revealed that he died a multi-millionaire, but only about $150,000 of his assets were made public knowledge as to their existence and intended beneficiaries. The reason that small fraction was public was because it was listed on forms in Mr. Rhodes' probate court file. Those particular assets were owned in his name individually. However, the vast majority of Mr. Rhodes' millions were owned by his trust. Since they were in trust, they avoided probate, so they were kept private. ("Former Gov. Rhodes Placed Most Assets in Trust," *The Columbus Dispatch,* Nov. 22, 2001). Mary remembered the news article she had seen a few years ago about probate files and wondered if she shouldn't look into a trust for her parents. No, she answered herself, her parents were of modest means, not millionaires. Still…did only the rich deserve privacy? Mary made a mental note to think about this later when she was not so busy.

It was as if the universe was trying to tell Mary something. Just two weeks later she ran across another article on this topic, this time from a Kentucky newspaper. The report was only a few column inches in size, barely large enough to notice. But it hit Mary like a two by four. This time reporters revealed that recently deceased NASCAR driver Dale Earnhardt willed several specific assets to his wife, but the information on the rest of his fortunes was kept private by the use of a trust. ("People: Earnhardt's Will Detailed," *Lexington Herald-Leader,* Dec. 6, 2001).

The third time's the charm. After seeing this third article, Mary decided she wanted to look into this idea of using a trust in an estate plan. If the idea didn't pan out for her parents, she might still be able to use the research for a WJM news segment. She had nothing on her calendar for today. She might as well take a nothing day and make it worthwhile. Mary tried to think of a famous deceased person in order to research his estate administration. Immediately she thought of one of her role models, Jacqueline Kennedy Onassis, who died in 1994. Mary turned to her computer and "Googled" Jackie O's full name followed by the words "last will and testament." Almost immediately she was given a link to the full text of Jackie's Will! The news producer in Mary thought this was great:

readily accessible information. The "private citizen" side of her thought, "you know, some things should just be kept private." Nevertheless, there was the Will on her screen, with a beautiful photo of Jackie, both hard to ignore. So Mary read Jackie's Will and learned that her hero left several pieces of artwork and historical memorabilia to specific persons and the JFK Library. She also sprinkled around some monetary gifts and family real estate. But the most relevant sections of the Will to Mary were those revealing that parts of the Kennedy family fortune were cloaked in two private trusts: one created by Jackie's first husband, President John F. Kennedy, and another, the "C & J Foundation," designed to avoid estate taxes and benefit the children of Carolyn and John, Jr.

That night when she was relaxing with Rhoda and Phyllis, Mary told the gals about her research and remarked that JFK must have had a trust way back in the 1950s or early 1960s, before his death in 1963. Phyllis responded, "Mary, were you born under a rock? Lars and I have had trusts for simply years!" Rhoda and Mary just laughed. But Mary decided right then and there that she needed to learn more about this topic for herself personally, as well as for her parents. Mary did some poking around and found there was an attorney in town giving free, educational trust workshops. She decided to attend. For a little moral support, she asked Georgette Franklin to join her for dinner and then the workshop. Sue Ann Nivens overheard them talking and invited herself along. Sue Ann figured there should be some eligible bachelors there. The ladies went to the workshop, absorbed a lot of good information, and left with even more information to read later. Mary's eyes were opened to the many advantages of using a revocable living trust for an estate plan, way more than just maintaining privacy. She made appointments for both herself and her parents so they could all upgrade their plans.

(The Mary Tyler Moore Show, 1970-1977)

A Good Plan: Mary Richards Makes It
After All—Was There Ever Any Doubt?

Everyone at the WJM-TV news department in Minneapolis knew that Mary Richards was an observant person. She noticed throughout her childhood and early adulthood that neglecting matters really cost you more in the end. So as an adult she formed good habits about things that affected her physical and financial well being. Twice a year she went to her dentist for a teeth cleaning and checkup. Once a year she had her eyes examined and went for a complete physical exam. Mary had the oil changed in her car at the recommended times. When she got her first home, she had her gutters cleaned every fall, and had her air conditioner serviced every spring. Every ten years she had her chimney cleaned of soot and the sewer lines cleaned of tree roots. Every fall Mary got a flu shot, trimmed back her rose bushes, and put new batteries in her smoke detectors. Once a year she took her dog to the vet for shots, and every month she gave her dog a heartworm pill.

So it should be no surprise to anyone that if Mary believed in the regular maintenance of her health, house, car and dog, that she wouldn't give her estate planning short shrift either. Mary was one smart cookie. She learned in that first trust workshop she attended many, many years ago, that there is a big difference between merely having legal estate planning *documents*, and having a comprehensive legal estate *plan*, a plan that actually works. She also learned that an estate plan needs to be *maintained*, just like any other aspect of your life. So Mary had regular "estate plan review" appointments with her estate planning attorney. Oh, at first, when she was in her 30's, and not much was changing in her finances or the circumstances surrounding her loved ones, she only went every five years or so. But as Mary grew older, she went more frequently. Mary knew all kinds of changes that happen in life can have an effect on her plan. Her assets changed as the stock market and real estate values did; as she grew older, Mary increased her assets by her own savings and by inheritance; the people she had selected to serve as her disability and death trustees, executors and attorneys in fact, or the alternate persons for each such position, moved, changed personalities or died; the law on powers of attorney and trusts changed; and legal thinking on proactive draftsmanship changed. All of these concepts made Mary and her attorney want to tweak her plan together periodically.

During one trust review appointment, Mary's attorney asked if she had received any stock as a result of the Prudential and Met Life demutualization processes. Why, yes she had! Not knowing what to do with those few shares when she received them, Mary sort of forgot about them. Mary's attorney explained that if Mary did nothing, those shares would remain outside Mary's trust and would need to be probated. The probate court costs were as much as the value of the few shares. Mary's attorney showed her how to transfer or sell the shares.

In another trust review appointment, Mary asked about a sunbelt vacation condo she had purchased to escape Minnesota winters. Mary and her attorney got that re-titled into Mary's trust so she wouldn't have a probate in a second state far away.

The next trip in to the lawyer, Mary learned that her state had revised its law on living wills and health care POAs. Mary got hers into compliance and updated her financial POA as well since it had aged to the point where some banks wouldn't accept it.

Mary's original beneficiaries in her trust were her several nieces and nephews. But later, one niece won the lottery, and one nephew married a heart surgeon with a patent on a surgical device. They were both quite wealthy and didn't need help as much as the rest of Mary's beneficiaries did. So in another trust review appointment, Mary changed her beneficiaries by a simple amendment. At that time she also added a charity she had not been familiar with in the prior decades of her life.

During yet another review, Mary discussed her concerns about a niece who had special needs. Originally Mary had not included her because an inheritance would disqualify her from state aid. Then when the niece's inheritance was gone, she might have trouble getting back on the program. But Mary's attorney explained that the law on special needs trusts had changed in the last few years. Mary was now able to set aside a percentage of her estate in a "safe harbor trust" for that niece. That brought Mary a tremendous amount of peace of mind. She sensed that's what estate planning is all about, namely *peace of mind*, not *pieces of paper*.

As Mary grew older, Mary's lawyer shared with her that attorneys around the country were adding new things to trusts. Legal draftsmanship had improved. As a result of the Baby Boomers and their parents experiencing age-related illnesses, attorneys were learning from their problems and including more trust clauses about the client's disability period. Mary opted for those amendments as well.

As Mary turned 65, she began to worry about an extended illness in her old age. Mary's attorney helped her segregate out and fund some of her assets to a separate "asset protection" trust. They also beefed up Mary's financial power of attorney to allow special actions that might become necessary in the event of Mary's long term illness. These clauses weren't automatically in the power of attorney Mary signed when she was in her 30's, because they involved giving up more control than Mary was ready for as a young woman. But now that she was in her mid 60's, the benefits outweighed the risks to Mary.

In her late 70's, Mary had a health emergency, like so many of us do. That was not a happy or welcome event, for sure. But because of the planning work Mary had done throughout her life, the situation was not as bad as it could have been. None of her family or friends had to run around in a panic about legalities, hospital rules, and finances. It was as if Mary had conducted life boat drills. Everyone just calmly proceeded to their stations. The life preservers and life boats were already there waiting in an orderly row. Mary had all her estate planning documents in order and people knew where to find them. The attorneys-in-fact named in Mary's POAs and the successor trustees of her trust were able to do what they were supposed to do. No one had to rush around and try to get in to see a lawyer at the last minute or have concerns about Mary's mental competence to sign any documents at that late date. Everyone could focus their attention solely on Mary's needs, and not on any distractions. Mary's planning made her final years and post-death legal processes more peaceful for Mary and less expensive and stressful for her loved ones. She was the epitome of a caring, responsible, and proactive woman. How'd that Mary get to be so smart? Let's follow her example!

(The Mary Tyler Moore Show, 1970-1977)

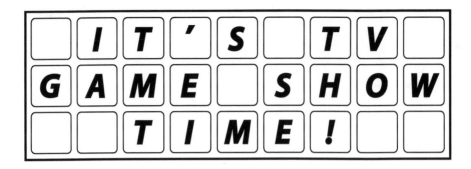

Announcer To Our Studio Audience:

Ladies and gentlemen, while the stage hands change the set during our commercial breaks, we have some additional prizes to award. Please listen carefully.

Question From Our TV Game Show Host:

For the outdoor gas grill cooking island, the trip to Aruba, and the opportunity to move on to our next round of elimination chapters, *can you name the 1950s-1970s TV shows in which the following catch phrases or lines were regularly said?* (The answers follow by corresponding question number.)

1. Goodnight, John-Boy.

2. Danger, Will Robinson! Danger, Danger!

3. Beam me up, Scotty.

4. Come on down!

5. I'd like to buy a vowel, Pat.

6. Same category for $1,000, Alex.

7. Bachelor No. 3

8. Making whoopee

9. The devil made me do it.

10. A one and a two…

11. And AWA-A-AY we go!

12. And that's the way it is.

13. De Plane, De Plane!

14. Shazam!, or Surprise, Surprise, Surprise!

15. I know nothing. I hear nothing. I see NOTHING!

16. One of these days… POW! Right in the kisser!

17. What's the matter? What is it, girl?
    Do you want us to follow you?

18. Just the facts, ma'am.

19. Hey, Grandpa, what's for dinner?,
    Just Call BR-549,
    Now it's time for Misty's bedtime stories, and
    So long, everybody! We'll see you next week on…
    (all from the same show)

20. Sock it to me, sock it to me, sock it to me!
    Here come de judge! Here come de judge!
    And that's the truth—plbbbbt!!
    You bet your sweet bippy.
    Blow in my ear and I'll follow you anywhere.
    Say goodnight, Dick.
    (all from the same show)

21. There is nothing wrong with your television set.
    Do not attempt to adjust the picture.

22. All smiles!

23. You are about to enter another dimension, a dimension not only of sight and sound, but of mind. A journey into a wondrous land of imagination. Next stop, the...

24. It's a really big shew tonight.

25. Attention all personnel, incoming choppers!

26. Kiss my grits!, or When donkeys fly!

27. Patience, grasshopper.

28. It's got a good beat and you can dance to it.

29. Smile, you're on...

30. Would you believe...

31. Dy-no-mite!

32. Que Sera, Sera, whatever will be, will be.

33. I got you, babe.

34. Book 'em, Danno, murder one.

35. Is it bigger than a bread box?

36. _____ (remember your own!)

37. _____

38. _____

39. _____

40. _____

Correct Answers From Our Panel of Judges:

1. The Waltons

2. Lost in Space

3. Star Trek

4. The Price Is Right

5. Wheel of Fortune

6. Jeopardy

7. The Dating Game

8. The Newlywed Game

9. The Flip Wilson Show

10. The Lawrence Welk Show

11. The Jackie Gleason Show

12. The CBS Evening News With Walter Cronkite

13. Fantasy Island

14. Gomer Pyle, USMC

15. Hogan's Heroes

16. The Honeymooners

17. Lassie

18. Dragnet

19. Hee Haw

20. Rowan and Martin's Laugh In

21. The Outer Limits

22. Sing Along With Mitch

23. The Twilight Zone

24. The Ed Sullivan Show

25. M*A*S*H (which stands for Mobile Army Surgical Hospital)

26. Both Alice and Flo

27. Kung Fu

28. American Bandstand

29. Candid Camera

30. Get Smart

31. Good Times

32. The Doris Day Show

33. Sonny and Cher Comedy Hour

34. Hawaii Five-O

35. What's My Line? (Steve Allen coined this.)

36. _____

37. _____

38. _____

39. _____

40. _____

Ginny Says

Did you wish you could have gone along with Mary Richards, and Georgette and Sue Ann, when they went to the workshop on revocable living trusts? Well as your TV studio tour guide, I went with them. How could I miss being in <u>that</u> car? I took notes at the workshop and I'll give you some of the high points here as I see them!

1. A "trust" is a relationship in which property is owned by one party for the benefit of another party. That relationship is often embodied in the form of a separate legal entity that can own property under the law (in that regard, it is like a corporation). It comes into life, or is created, when a contract, or "trust agreement," is fully signed. That contract is signed by two parties, namely a Trustmaker (person creating the trust) and a Trustee (person being entrusted to manage the trust property). There is a third identity involved in the trust arrangement, but it does not necessarily have to be a "signing party." That third identity is the group of one or more persons (for example, you and/or people you care about) or entities (for example churches, colleges or other charities or institutions) who are meant to benefit from the trust. They are called Beneficiaries. So there are three identities involved in a Trust: Trustmaker(s), Trustee(s) and Beneficiary(ies).

2. Trusts have existed for thousands of years, since at least the time of ancient Rome. Knights in the Middle Ages used them so someone could legally manage their property on their behalf while the Knights were out on the Crusades. From that era evolved

the legal distinctions of legal and equitable ownership of property. For hundreds of years the three trust identities were often separate. For example, maybe an older Rockefeller was a Trustmaker, and he used a big bank as the Trustee, for the best interests of his grandchildren, the Beneficiaries. But then law evolved and that separation of identities was no longer necessary. Now one person can wear all three hats. So you can be the Trustmaker, your own Trustee, and the primary beneficiary while you are living. That's pretty neat, don't you think? That evolution is what made the trust concept palatable to middle class Americans who could still remember the Great Depression. Otherwise, they would not "trust" a bank to "own" their money! As long as they could retain *control,* these clients embraced the idea of using a trust for their estate plan.

3. That was all interesting, but maybe it was more than I needed to know. *Here* is where it got relevant to me. The workshop speaker said there are all kinds of trusts: revocable trusts, where you can always change your mind, and irrevocable trusts, where you can't always do so; living trusts (made while you are alive) and testamentary trusts (created by your last will and "testament" after your death). There are many more types, but the point of this workshop was to explain the benefits of Revocable Living Trusts, or RLT's, so that's where I really took notes. Here are just some of the advantages of a Revocable Living Trust over a "Simple Will":

    - Wills only take effect at death. Living trusts are also beneficial during your lifetime, as a plan for your time of illness or disability, to avoid having to submit to court control and choices for you. I don't know about you, but I think what happens to *me* and *my family* during illness should be more important to me than what happens to my *money* after I'm dead!

    - Living trusts can avoid the risks of asset loss and lack of stepped-up basis for joint ownership of assets and other poor substitutes for good estate planning.

    - If you have minor children or grandchildren who might inherit, a trust can avoid a costly and cumbersome guardianship for them until age 18 and then inheritance dumping on them at age 18.

- If you have a spouse, you can avoid how simple Wills waste one estate tax exemption, thus reducing federal and state estate taxes, if applicable.

- Trusts can be used to dole out money over time to beneficiaries (even adults), instead of dumping inheritance on them, helping protect them from their own mistakes, as well as their spouses, children, in-laws, predators and creditors.

- Trusts can provide for special circumstances, like special needs heirs, second marriages, children from prior marriages, family property or businesses, charities, large life insurance policies, pets and animals, and much more!

- Trusts can be used to plan for the well being of loved ones after your death, such as an aging spouse, or others who need protection.

- Trusts are used to avoid having to probate assets through the court system to transfer title, thus:

    - Reducing possible delays.
    - Avoiding "Will Contests".
    - Avoiding asset, debt and beneficiary information being a public record.
    - Avoiding probate attorney and executor fees.
    - Avoiding two probates—one in my home state and one for my out of state property.

The workshop speaker made the point that probate in and of itself is not all bad, and he wasn't necessarily promoting the use of trusts solely for that purpose. He pointed out there are certain situations where a probate may be exactly what is needed—court supervision. He suggested that what is important is to look at each client's individual circumstances and overall goals. After that my notes trail off. I think the cookies were being passed. There was more to it, but this should at least make you aware of enough issues to cause you to investigate the estate planning options in your home state!

Notes

_____

_____

_____

_____

_____

_____

_____

_____

_____

_____

_____

_____

_____

_____

_____

Part Five

Even Better Plans!

Jed Clampett Leaves A Legacy Beyond His Kin:
Charitable Remainder Trusts (CRTs)

Most people thought Jed Clampett was just a poor mountaineer who could barely feed his family, until one day he discovered oil while rabbit hunting. But Jed was seriously misunderstood. Underneath that worn and tattered hat was a thinker. Jed was a keen observer of the human condition and a planner for the future. He *had* to plan year round in the past just to make sure they had food! He wasn't going to stop thinking ahead now just because he was filthy rich.

Jed knew he could support Granny in style for the rest of her life. Daisy May would *never* have to worry about how to buy parts for her moonshine still! But he worried about the generation who would outlive him, namely Jethro and Elly May. He reckoned gold diggers and gigolos would cheat them out of *their* inheritance. Jed had also taken a shine to Miss Jane. He reckoned Mr. Drysdale seriously underpaid her. She probably would never be able to retire without assistance. Jed wanted to do something to help out all three of them after his death. He sat on the curb in his britches with Duke and whittled while he chewed on this riddle. Finally, without telling her of his plan, Jed asked Miss Jane to find him the best down-home style family lawyer in Beverly Hills. Miss Jane knew he needed someone a little different from that, and she found him the right attorney, one concentrating her law practice exclusively in estate planning and supporting areas.

Jed met with Miss Jane's referral and described the situation. They talked for a long time. The attorney promised she would get back to Jed with some recommendations in a few weeks. She did just that, proposing ways to not only protect and provide for Jed's kinfolk, but to save estate taxes. Jed looked at the various options she explained and selected a "CRT," which is an acronym for a "charitable remainder trust." The attorney had done calculations showing Jed how much income Jed's black gold millions could reasonably make per year after his death. It was more than enough to support Jethro, Elly May, and Jane Hathaway in style for the rest of their lives! They'd never want for vittles, or anything else. After all three of them died, the principal amount left over in trust would go to charities of Jed's choosing. This got Jed a charitable deduction, so his estate would not be ravaged by estate taxes. Jed's attorney had explained to him that estate taxes are *optional* with good planning, so he decided to opt out. If his money was going to be taken as a tax and redistributed as "social capital," *he'd* rather decide where it went rather than let Congress do it. With the CRT, Jed could provide for his kin, preserve his estate, AND help causes that were meaningful to Jed. *Well, doggies!* Jed was as pleased as punch with this plan. He felt such a huge sense of relief knowing his affairs were in order.

After all the papers were signed, Jed felt it was a cause for celebration. He invited that estate planning attorney over for a BBQ around the cement pond. Jed wound up going to see her every three years to review his plan and keep it tuned up. In one of those meetings, Jed learned you don't have to be rich to use a CRT to take care of someone. CRTs can be funded with much smaller amounts of money than Jed had.

In fact, Jed learned something new at every visit. His lawyer kept him informed on changes in the law and new developments in attorney thinking and tools. Jed sure was glad he had an ongoing *relationship* with an estate planning attorney instead of just going to her for a *one-time transaction*. This estate planning attorney became an important part of his life, like his doctor, his dentist, Miss Jane… and even Mr. Drysdale. In fact, Jed liked her so much, he was thinking about giving her the 1922 Olds flatbed truck that he and the family had driven to California. He reckoned if she replaced the old piece of rope that held it together, it would work just fine for many more years to come. He was in a grand mood now. California really <u>was</u> the place to be!

(Beverly Hillbillies, 1962-1971)

Dr. Ben Casey Gets A Better Prescription Than Dr. James Kildare: Irrevocable Life Insurance Trusts (ILITs)

In 1962 Blair General Hospital sent Dr. James Kildare to a medical conference. He introduced himself to the young doctor seated next to him, a Dr. Ben Casey from County General Hospital. The first conference lecture was quite interesting, but the second was not. Both doctors' minds started to wander. Dr. Kildare wondered if he had been a ship's navigator en route to Japan in another life, or perhaps a priest living near a sheep ranch in the Australian outback. Dr. Casey just doodled on his clipboard. He seemed to be designing wallpaper with symbols for man, woman, birth, death and infinity.

Luckily lunch time arrived. Back to reality. As the handsome pair headed to the dining hall, they passed by the convention vendors and picked up brochures at the life insurance booth. Over lunch the two doctors commiserated on how deeply in debt they were from their years of education and training. They agreed that some day they wanted to leave their respective hospitals and set up private practices. That would require *more* debt. They hoped that at some point they'd find wives and have children. They worried about what would happen to their families if they died with all those loans unpaid. Even if the debts were paid off by the time of their deaths, they worried how their families would continue to live in the style to which they had become accustomed if their bread winner was gone. They wanted their children to be able to obtain post-graduate educations like they had done. The good doctors chatted some more. Finally James and Ben challenged each other to buy $2 million in life insurance when they returned to their respective homes.

Dr. Kildare did as promised. The insurance agent made Dr. Kildare the owner of the policy, with Dr. Kildare's trust as the beneficiary. That was a good *distribution* plan, as James could rather simply revise the beneficiaries of his trust as his circumstances changed through the years, as opposed to changing the beneficiary designation on the insurance. Also, the trust could provide for how the money would be used in much more detail and with more contingencies than a mere beneficiary form could provide. Lastly, the trust could pay James' debts "off the top" from the insurance proceeds, before dividing up the balance for the trust beneficiaries. The problem is that Dr. Kildare didn't call his trust lawyer about this new part of his estate plan, so he didn't realize he had made a BIG mistake in the *way* that he purchased this insurance.

Dr. Casey followed up on their insurance pact as well, but he first discussed the matter with his mentor, Dr. David Zorba. "Life insurance is a great idea for you," David told him, "but you better talk to my estate planning attorney about how it affects your *taxes*."

"But this brochure says life insurance proceeds aren't taxable," Ben objected. Dr. Zorba didn't believe that was the *full* story. He convinced Ben to at least go talk to his attorney before Ben signed the insurance application. Ben did so and was surprised to learn that while life insurance proceeds aren't *income* taxed, they *are estate* taxed. True, if Ben died in debt, the debt would be a deduction reducing some of that tax. But Ben was shocked to be told that if he died with his debts paid off, up to 77 percent of the life insurance proceeds would be taken in federal estate taxes! There wouldn't be enough left to accomplish his other purposes. Luckily Ben was in the right place. Dr. Zorba's estate planning attorney explained to Dr. Casey that the estate taxation on life insurance could be <u>avoided</u> by the use of an ILIT ("Irrevocable Life Insurance Trust") or some other legal planning. Dr. Casey never knew some taxes are *optional* with proper planning. He was glad he found the right estate planning "prescription."

(Dr. Kildare, 1961-1966; Ben Casey, 1961-1966)

Announcer To Our Studio Audience:

If you have or want a large amount of life insurance to pay debt and taxes, support your loved ones, or accomplish the buy-out of a family business interest, please discuss with an experienced estate planning attorney how that impacts your overall plan. State estate taxation varies from state to state. The federal estate tax system has been changing dramatically the last few years. It is important to stay current on its effect upon you. On the following page is a chart of historical federal estate tax exemptions and rates. This chart illustrates the magnitude of estate taxation and the frequency with which the laws can change. _What will the tax law be in the year you die?_ Since we can't know that answer many years in advance, only an up to date plan can accomplish your goals. _How old is your plan?_

As you review the chart on the next page, remember, Congress can always change the law! It is important to have an ongoing relationship with your estate planning attorney and to periodically have your plan compared not only to the current law, but to evolving thoughts on legal draftsmanship.

HISTORICAL FEDERAL ESTATE TAX		
Year of Death	Amount Estate Tax Exempt	Top Tax Rate
1942-1976	$60,000	77%
1977	$120,000	70%
1978	$134,000	70%
1979	$147,000	70%
1980	$161,000	70%
1981	$175,000	70%
1982	$225,000	65%
1983	$275,000	60%
1984	$325,000	55%
1985	$400,000	55%
1986	$500,000	55%
1987-1997	$600,000	55%
1998	$625,000	55%
1999	$650,000	55%
2000-2001	$675,000	55%
2002	$1,000,000	50%
2003	$1,000,000	49%
2004	$1,500,000	48%
2005	$1,500,000	47%
2006	$2,000,000	46%
2007-2008	$2,000,000	45%
2009	$3,500,000	45%
2010	N/A—repealed	N/A
2011	$5,000,000	35%
2012	$5,120,000	35%
2013	$5,250,000	40%
2014+	Call Chris or Debbie!	419-891-8884

Ben Cartwright Preserves the Ponderosa
(FLPs, LLCs, Family Trusts & Subchapter S Corps)

Ben Cartwright ran his hands through his silver hair in desperation. All over the dining room table and surrounding chairs, sideboards, and serving carts were strewn assorted maps of parts of the Ponderosa—all 600,000 acres of it. Hop Sing looked in on Ben once in a while to see if he wanted coffee or anything. This time he just stood in the doorway, silently assessing the carnage. He knew by Ben's slumped shoulders and very rare look of surrender that things had gotten pretty ugly.

The whole mess had started yesterday when word came that the Ponderosa had revealed yet another of its riches. Gold had been discovered in the northwest 40 acres of the southeast quadrant! That night at the dinner table Adam, Hoss and Little Joe spoke excitedly about the find and bantered about the best way to handle the mining operation and the proceeds. Good natured differences of opinion turned into a heated argument. Ben wished the boys were still young enough to send to their rooms without dessert, but it had been a long time since anyone in the house could get between Hoss and a pie. Ben left them arguing and went out to the porch for some fresh air and a look at the stars. As he leaned against a porch post, up rode Sheriff Roy Coffee and Deputy Clem Foster. They came to tell Ben that one of his good friends had been shot dead and to enlist the three Cartwright boys for a search posse tomorrow.

The next day after an early breakfast, the boys saddled up and rode out. Ben quickly dug out all the maps for his project. All night long he had been thinking about the death of his friend, and it made him think of all the people he'd lost through the years in this Nevada. When he thought about how he had survived three wives, the English, Swedish and French Creole mothers of Adam, Hoss and Joseph respectively, Ben got to wondering how much longer he'd be around. He resolved to start getting his affairs in order as soon as he had the house to himself in the morning.

Ben's plan was to look at the maps and figure a way to divide up the Ponderosa into three 200,000 acre parcels, one for each son. He was still hoping the boys would find wives and give him some grandchildren some day. They couldn't all live in one house, so they'd want to move to different sections and build their own homes. If Ben divided the land up while he was still living, there should be less arguing. In fact, maybe he'd have the boys draw straws to pick their parcel.

Ben uncurled all the maps and weighted them down with cups and bowls. As soon as he started looking for landmarks to give the surveyors for the parcel splits, he knew he had a problem. There didn't seem to be an obvious way to cut the Ponderosa into three pieces that were of equal acres or equal value. Some land was tillable with good soil for crops. Some was not—too rocky and alkaline. Some land was good for livestock grazing. Some was not—too hilly. Some had timber ready for harvest. Other timber areas wouldn't be ready for another 20 years. Some land bordered on beautiful Lake Tahoe. Ben could see his architect son, Adam, wanting to build houses all around it for resale, and the other boys wanting to keep the area private. Plus they'd all three want that fishing cabin up there! Other land had no natural water source. Some land had access to roads and trails. Other parts were completely landlocked. Some sections of the Ponderosa were good for hunting and trapping, while the rest weren't. One little strip had some pretty productive oil and gas wells. Now gold had been discovered! How many more secrets did the Ponderosa have that would affect its future value as to particular sections? How in the world could Ben possibly divide this *bonanza* of known and unknown riches equally among his three sons? The task seemed impossible. Give Ben a physical job, or one of advice or diplomacy, and no man was his match. But this conceptual stuff? Your foe is invisible. There was nothing to shoot at or punch. Ben desperately wanted to leave his sons set up for success, not arguments. Most of all, he wanted their family business to continue for generations to come. He didn't want the land divided up to risk pieces of it being sold off. Ben was filled with despair.

It was at this point that Hop Sing came and stood in the doorway to the dining room. After a few seconds, Hop Sing asked Ben what the trouble was. Ben gave him a brief recap. Hop Sing got it right away, because he had seen the tempers flare between the boys and knew their differing interests. Hop Sing asked Ben, "Why not ask your friend's widow what she is doing with her Big Valley? She must have the same problem, especially now that she knows her husband left an illegitimate son. When she is gone, how will her children treat *him*? And the Big Valley?"

Hop Sing was referring to Victoria Barkley and her children Jarrod, Nick, and Audra, and the new son on the scene, Heath. Now that he thought about it, Ben agreed that Victoria probably did have some fancy California lawyer all over her situation. What a great idea! Ben was so used to being the go-to guy, he never thought of seeking help. Ben put the maps away and wrote Victoria a letter. He rode in to Virginia City to post it that very day.

By return mail (which took about a month back then), Ben Cartwright got a response letter from Victoria Barkley. She *had* been to see an estate planning attorney about this same issue for *her* family property. Apparently there are several ways to handle this without having to physically carve up the land into smaller parcels. The property could remain as one huge parcel if it were owned *by a legal entity*, such as an FLP (family limited partnership), LLC (limited liability company), family trust, or Subchapter S corporation. The company could be run by the boys with equal votes. If they wanted, some areas of the Ponderosa could be set aside for conservation and shared family recreation. Some areas could be allocated for their use for personal homesteads. But every other area could be put to its natural highest and best use and maximum productivity. All profits would pour into one account and subsequently be paid out in three equal shares. As grandchildren appeared and reached adulthood, they could be brought into the company as either voting or nonvoting members with participation in profits. The Ponderosa could stay intact and be passed on as a Cartwright legacy for years to come. Ben felt a tremendous sense to know his problem could be solved with the right specialized legal help. His "map meltdown" had accomplished something after all!

Announcer To Our Studio Audience:

In the movie sequel, Ben's granddaughters multiply the Cartwright fortunes by negotiating cell tower leases on the Ponderosa, as well as establishing a dude ranch, tourist fishing camp, hot springs spa, and Alpaca ranch!

(Bonanza, 1959-1973; The Big Valley, 1965-1969)

The Animal Bloopers—We're Family, Too! (Pet Trusts)

Our favorite animal television stars lived wonderful lives during the height of their TV show ratings. Rin Tin Tin, Lassie, Flipper, Gentle Ben—they all received the best food, shelter and medical care available, plus regular grooming, exercise, affection and training from their caregivers. They were kept safe from guns, vehicles, and machinery. Stunt doubles performed their dangerous scenes. Maybe it was that pampered lifestyle that contributed to their longevity, but several of our furry, finned and feathered TV heroes outlived their human co-stars. Once their co-stars were gone, their quality of life went downhill fast!

As just one example of the potential situation, remember Wilbur Post and his three-year-old palomino, "Mister Ed"? A horse, *of course*, can live 40 years or more. Imagine Wilbur and his wife, Carol, were killed in a car accident a year after taking on Mister Ed. Imagine they left no estate plan, or left an incomplete one that did not contain directions for Mister Ed. What happens to Mister Ed for the next 36 years?

Some might call this line of thought silly. But a dog loving author who happens to be an estate planning attorney says *"take your motivation wherever you find it."* If your thirty year high school class reunion is what finally makes you stick to a diet, fine. If the realization that your beloved animal companion will be at risk upon your disability or death finally motivates you to get a great estate plan designed or updated, your attorney and family should have the horse sense to just be grateful and not poke fun.

As it turned out, Wilbur Post actually did have a plan for Mister Ed. Mister Ed had worried about his future and pestered Wilbur into going to see a friend of his, Marlin Perkins, host of "Mutual of Omaha's 'Wild Kingdom'." Marlin referred Wilbur to his own personal estate planning attorney. Wilbur Post got a masterful plan for himself and Carol, as well as a Pet Trust that took care of Mister Ed in the event Wilbur became seriously ill or died. Way to go, Mister Ed and Marlin!

(Adventures of Rin Tin Tin, 1954-1959; Lassie, 1954-1973; Flipper, 1964-1967; Gentle Ben, 1967-1969; Mister Ed, 1961-1966; Mutual of Omaha's 'Wild Kingdom', 1963-1988)

Notes

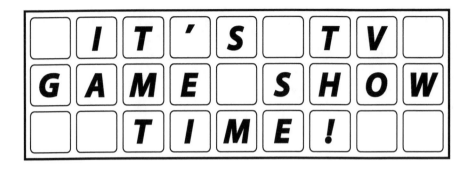

Announcer To Our Studio Audience:

Ladies and gentlemen, while our producers get ready to acknowledge the companies who provided promotional considerations for our shows, we have some additional contest prizes to award. Please listen carefully.

Question From Our TV Game Show Host:

For the stainless steel kitchen appliance set, the trip to Cancun, and the opportunity to move on to our Bonus Round appearing after the Glossary, *can you name these 1950s-1970s TV show stars or characters?* (The answers follow by corresponding question number.)

1. Who wore a tuxedo, drank scotch and smoked cigarettes on camera during his show?

2. Who made cardigan sweaters all the rage with men for a while?

3. Which two characters were notoriously bad at making coffee?

4. Who hosted friends Vicki Lawrence, Harvey Korman, Tim Conway, and Lyle Waggoner?

5. Name at least three popular comedians of the 1950s-1970s, whether in reruns, established or just getting started.

6. What same character appeared on three different TV series over 20 years (tying the 20 year record of Matt Dillon and Doc Adams for longevity)?

7. Who starred in three popular TV series almost nonstop from 1959 to 1989 and appeared on the cover of TV Guide 22 times (second only to Lucille Ball), yet was never awarded an Emmy before death at age 54?

8. Who starred in My Favorite Martian, The Courtship of Eddie's Father, The Magician, and The Incredible Hulk, as well as movies and game shows?

9. Who played a mother figure in Lassie, Lost in Space, and Petticoat Junction?

10. Who starred in three sit-com series featuring parts of his real name in the titles? (Hint: The entire second series was just a dream.)

11. Who played Fred and Bub on two different shows?

12. Who started out in radio as a child, then played the same character on TV from 1952-1966, ending episodes with a song after 1957, and later having 20 top-ten Billboard hits?

13. Many TV shows featured people in law enforcement, espionage, law, medicine, science and science fiction. Name some shows in which main characters were *architects.*

14. Who created and played George Appleby, Gertrude and Heathcliff, Sheriff Deadeye, San Fernando Red, Cauliflower McPugg, The Mean Widdle Kid, Clem Kadiddlehopper, and Freddie the Freeloader?

15. What were the character names of the very mod trio who were advertised as "a white, a black and a blonde?"

16. Who said "Good night and good news." as his sign off?

17. Who said "Good day and may the good news be yours." as his sign off?

18. Who encouraged spay/neuter of pets at the end of every show?

19. What actor played the revolver-toting San Francisco paladin who "advertised" with a calling card that displayed his name and a white knight chess piece?

20. What character went to jail as the way his series was ended?

21. Whose dialog was always extreme slang, sometimes barely understandable?

22. Who arranged a Marilyn Monroe TV appearance in a 1953 skit on his show?

23. What uncle was credited for the sales of millions of TV sets?

24. Who did a tango with eggs in her shirt and made a Vitameatavegamin commercial under its influence?

25. What actors portrayed tennis players who were really undercover secret agents?

26. What undercover secret agent was appointed by Ulysses S. Grant?

27. Who was a bald lollipop lover?

28. What earlier character helped inspire the later show known as "The X-Files"?

29. _____ (remember your own!)

30. _____

31. _____

32. _____

33. _____

Correct Answers From Our Panel of Judges:

1. Dean Martin

2. Perry Como

3. Lisa Douglas (from Green Acres), and Detective Nick Yemana (from Barney Miller)

4. Carol Burnett

5. Dom DeLouise, Paul Lynde, Don Rickles, Phyllis Diller, Totie Fields, Moms Mabley, Jerry Lewis and Dean Martin, Jack Benny, George Burns and Gracie Allen, George Carlin, Flip Wilson, Groucho Marx, Bob Hope and Bing Crosby, Bill Cosby, Bob Newhart, Robin Williams, Alan King, Woody Allen, Charlie Chaplin, Abbot and Costello, Jonathan Winters, Rich Little, and W.C. Fields, as just a few.

6. Frasier Crane (in Cheers, Frasier, and Wings)

7. Michael Landon (in Bonanza, Little House on the Prairie, and Highway to Heaven)

8. Bill Bixby

9. June Lockhart

10. Bob Newhart (in The Bob Newhart Show, Newhart, and Bob)

11. William Frawley (in I Love Lucy and My Three Sons)

12. Ricky Nelson (in The Adventures of Ozzie and Harriet)

13. Bonanza (Adam Cartwright), The Invaders (David Vincent), Mister Ed (Wilbur Post), and The Brady Bunch (Mike Brady)

14. Red Skelton

15. Pete, Linc and Julie (The Mod Squad)

16. Ted Baxter (The Mary Tyler Moore Show)

17. Les Nessman (WKRP in Cincinnati)

18. Bob Barker (The Price is Right)

19. Richard Boone (Have Gun, Will Travel)

20. Sgt. Ernie Bilko

21. Kookie (77 Sunset Strip)

22. Jack Benny

23. Milton Berle (Uncle Miltie)

24. Lucy Ricardo (Lucille Ball)

25. Robert Culp and Bill Cosby (in I Spy)

26. James T. West (in The Wild, Wild West)

27. Kojak

28. Reporter Carl Kolchak

29. _____

30. _____

31. _____

32. _____

33. _____

Ginny Says

We hope Mary Richards' story has convinced you that your legal estate plan is not something you should do once and then never revisit. You'll need a tune-up regularly, and even a complete overhaul once in a while. Along those lines, we also encourage you to meet with your other professionals on a regular basis. Who do we mean by that? Those professionals whose advice can also affect the long term success of your estate plan.

1. **Schedule Regular Review Appointments With Your Property and Casualty Insurer.** As one example, if your house burns down under-insured for replacement value, your finances—meaning your estate—will be seriously affected! Or if you declined the car rental insurance on vacation, because you weren't sure what to do, and then had a major accident, your estate can be affected. Please call your insurer and ask him or her how often you need to meet to discuss your coverage. He or she would love to hear from you when it is not about your fender bender or the tree in your roof! Discuss and agree on the frequency of meetings, and make ticklers on your calendar to follow up.

2. **Schedule Regular Review Appointments With Your Financial Planner.** This is absolutely critical. As attorneys, more and more we are seeing people trying to retire with nowhere near enough in savings and investments to sustain them. With today's rapidly changing financial markets and economy, it is more important than ever to keep an eye on how your investments are allocated for risk, growth and

income, and to get professional and thorough advice. If you don't have a *personal* relationship with a financial planner or advisor (meaning *not* an 800 number or an online stock account), please ask your estate planning attorney to recommend one to you. Meeting once a year is not too often. Your particular investments might require monitoring more often, especially as your goals and objectives change over time.

3. **Think Over Your Relationship With Your CPA or Tax Return Preparer**. Do you only talk every year in March or April? Does he or she just prepare your returns or help you plan ahead? Every chapter in your life presents different tax opportunities that you can't afford to miss. Please ask your tax professional what month of the year is a good one to chat, look at your year-to-date paystubs or other data, and plan ways to save taxes. Ask him or her how frequently you two should meet. Again, mark it down and follow up.

4. **Consider Preplanning Your Funeral.** As attorneys, we almost always ask our clients who are in their 60's and 70's if they have preplanned their funeral. Unfortunately, many don't or won't, unless it is part of a Medicaid spend down situation. The client's first objection is the cost. Understandably, he doesn't want to spend money currently on something he hopes won't be needed for years. But did you know that you can go preplan your funeral without prepaying? Just go pick out what you want done and not done! Get that much out of the way for your loved ones, as well as giving the funeral director the background data for your obituary and death certificate so they are accurate.

So you don't have to pay, NOW what is your excuse? Well…you don't like to think about dying. Understood. But imagine how your family will be forced into making the myriad of decisions necessary when you die, and what that will put them through at the worst time in their life. Wouldn't you rather decide now so *you* are in control and there is nothing for your family to guess (or argue) about in that regard? In all our years of experience meeting with the spouse or children of decedents, not ONE of them ever said "Gee, I really wish mom hadn't spared me all the stress and anxiety of picking out all her funeral arrangements." Instead, EVERY single person, whose loved one preplanned, said something along these lines: "You know, mom's final gift to me was taking care of all those decisions for us. My brother thought she wanted an open casket and a burial. My sister thought she wanted family visitation but cremation. Then we found out mom had it all decided and arranged. I'll never forget what a kindness that was to all of us. She allowed us to have time to just think and pray and reflect on the good memories." *Now isn't that what <u>you</u> want for your loved ones?*

If another objection you have to preplanning is that you don't want to go to a meeting at a funeral home, please call and ask if the preplanner makes house or business calls! If you are worried that the funeral home may go out of business after you pay in full or you start a regular payment plan, also ask how the money is handled. Funeral homes frequently utilize an insurance company to provide you with a policy for this purpose, so you have more protection. (That would also allow your funeral to take place in another city or state in case you move before death.) Do you still have more objections or questions? Please consult your estate planning attorney!

My Action Plan

☐ Spread the word to my parents, siblings, spouse, children, friends or others about the perils of self-help, procrastination, neglect, fill-in-the-blank forms, do-it-yourself kits, the internet, second hand "advice", listening to non-attorneys, or getting estate planning advice or documents from attorneys who don't concentrate in estate planning. (Should I give them a copy of this book?)

☐ Schedule an appointment to attend an estate planning workshop or to meet with an estate planning attorney to implement a new estate plan or review and/or update an old one.

☐ Review the information on the prior two pages about calling my property and casualty insurer, financial planner, and CPA or tax return preparer and take appropriate action.

☐ Consider preplanning my funeral so that my wishes are made known.

Other: _____

_____

_____

Epilogue on Long Term Care

No conversation about estate planning and elder law is complete without mention of the VA Pension for the long term care of wartime veterans or their surviving spouses. Although this benefit has been around for years, it is only within the last decade that its availability has become general public knowledge. Also the VA has only been accrediting attorneys in this area of practice since 2008.

If you or someone you love is a U.S. veteran from a *time* of war (regardless of geographic *location* of military service), or is the surviving spouse of such a veteran, please be aware that a Veteran's benefit may be available, called the "VA Pension" or the "VA Aid and Attendance Benefit." Its purpose is to provide monthly tax-free reimbursement for the private pay expenses of nursing home care, assisted living care, or regular in-home care, within certain limits.

If you are interested in further information on Medicaid coverage or the VA Pension, please speak with an elder law and estate planning attorney in your home state. A few years ago the Medicaid look back period was lengthened from three to five years. It could be expanded again in the future. Procrastination in planning can be a very costly mistake in all areas, but especially those impacting your long term care.

Definition of Estate Planning

We believe "estate planning" should be defined as follows:

"I want to control my property while I'm alive.

I want to take care of myself and my loved ones if I become incapacitated.

I want to give what I have, to whom I want, the way that I want, when I want, and with privacy.

I want to save every last tax dollar, professional fee, and court cost possible.

I want the legacy I leave to be more than just about money.

I want a plan that works!"

Please read that definition again and ask yourself if that isn't what you also want. Now does <u>your</u> current estate plan accomplish all that?

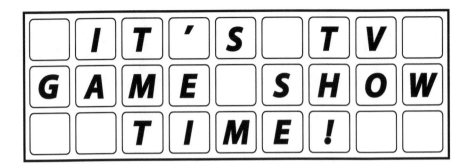

Bonus Round!

Announcer To Our Studio Audience:

Ladies and gentlemen, to reward you for being so patient with all the legal scenarios, we provide you one last round of TV trivia fun.

Question From Our TV Game Show Host:

For the Shetland Pony, the home theater system, the Alaska railway/cruise trip, and the satisfaction of completing this final round, *can you name the 1950s-1970s TV show in which each of the following gestures or physical actions by a character was regularly featured, in some cases in every episode?* (The answers follow by corresponding question number.)

1. Woman tugging her earlobe

2. Woman winking at her reflection in a store window

3. Young man holding a thumbs up

4. Woman powerfully wrinkling her nose to and fro

5. Man in a suit swinging an imaginary golf club

6. Forearm raised, palm facing forward, fingers split three and two

7. Woman folding arms across chest, nodding and blinking

8. A man hood slidin'

9. Woman saying "Mmmm-WAH!" and blowing a kiss off her palm to the audience

10. Woman tossing her beret in the air and looking up

11. Man pratfalling over an ottoman after walking in the front door of his home

12. Brandishing a sword to create cuts in the shape of the last alphabet letter

13. Getting his horse to stand up on its back two legs with him in the saddle

14. Rapidly spinning to transform Diana Prince into...

15. Tilting her head just right so her heavily starched cornette could catch a passing San Juan breeze

16. Racing into a telephone booth to change clothes

17. Holding an envelope to his turban covered head in order to divine the answer to a question written on a card sealed in the envelope.

18. _____ (remember your own!)

19. _____

20. _____

21. _____

22. _____

Correct Answers From Our Panel of Judges:

1. The Carol Burnett Show

2. That Girl

3. Happy Days

4. Bewitched

5. The Tonight Show Starring Johnny Carson

6. Star Trek

7. I Dream of Jeannie

8. The Dukes of Hazzard

9. The Dinah Shore Show

10. The Mary Tyler Moore Show

11. The Dick Van Dyke Show

12. Zorro

13. The Lone Ranger

14. Wonder Woman

15. The Flying Nun

16. Superman

17. The Tonight Show Starring Johnny Carson (Carnac the Magnificent)

18. _____

19. _____

20. _____

21. _____

22. _____

Folks, you've been a great audience.
Thanks for tuning in!

Index

For Your Nostalgic Amusement,

MEMORABLE 1950s-1970s TV SHOWS

The Game Shows

(Notable years and hosts are listed, but this list is not all inclusive. There were other shows, and many of these also appeared during several additional time periods with other hosts or in different versions or under different names. Several were preceded by radio versions.)

Concentration, 1958-59, Hugh Downs

I've Got a Secret, 1952-64, Garry Moore; 1964-67, Steve Allen

Jeopardy, 1964-75 & 78-79, Art Fleming; 1984-today, Alex Trebek

Let's Make a Deal, 1963-77 & other years, Monty Hall

Name That Tune, 1953-85, on and off, seven hosts

Password, 1961-67 & 1971-75, Allen Ludden

People Are Funny, 1954-1960, Art Linkletter

Queen For A Day, 1956-64, Jack Bailey

The $64,000 Question, 1955-58, Hal March

The Dating Game, 1965-73+, Jim Lange

The Hollywood Squares, 1966-81, Peter Marshall

The Newlywed Game, 1966-74, Bob Eubanks, many reprisals

The Price is Right, 1956-65, Bill Cullen; 1972-2007, Bob Barker

To Tell The Truth, 1956-68, Bud Collyer

Truth or Consequences, 1950-78 (Bob Barker 1956-75)

What's My Line?, 1950-67, John Charles Daly

Wheel of Fortune

Daytime, Chuck Woolery/Susan Stafford   1975-91
Evening, Pat Sajak/Vanna White   1983-present

You Bet Your Life, 1950-61, Groucho Marx

The Variety, Comedy & Talk Shows

Andy Williams Show	1959-1971
Art Linkletter's House Party	1952-1969
Arthur Godfrey's Talent Scouts/Friends	1948-1958
Bing Crosby Show	1964-1965
Bob Hope Shows and Specials	1950-1996
Caesar's Hour	1954-1957
Carol Burnett Show	1967-1978
Colgate Comedy Hour	1950-1955
Danny Kaye Show	1963-1967
Dean Martin Show	1965-1974
Dinah Shore Show	1951-1956
Donald O'Connor Show	1954-1955
Donny and Marie Show	1976-1979
Ed Sullivan Show/Toast of the Town	1948-1971
Fireside Theater	1949-1958
Flip Wilson Show	1970-1974
Garry Moore Show(s)	1950-1967
George Gobel Show	1954-1960
Glen Campbell Goodtime Hour	1969-1972
Hee Haw	1969-1992
Hollywood Palace	1964-1970
Hootenanny	1963-1964

Hullabaloo	1965-1966
Jack Benny Program	1950-1965
Jackie Gleason Show(s)	1952-1970
Jim Nabors Hour	1969-1971
Jimmy Durante Show	1954-1956
Joey Bishop Show	1967-1969
Johnny Cash Show	1969-1971
Judy Garland Show	1963-1964
Julie Andrews Hour	1972-1973
Lawrence Welk Show	1955-1982
Martha Raye Show	1954-1956
Merv Griffin Show	1962-1986
Milton Berle Show/Texaco Star Theater	1948-1956
Nat King Cole Show	1956-1957
Perry Como, Various Shows & Specials	1948-1994
Red Buttons Show	1952-1955
Red Skelton Show	1951-1971
Rowan and Martin's Laugh In	1968-1973
Sammy Davis, Jr., Show	1966
Shindig	1964-1966
Shower of Stars	1954-1958
Sing Along With Mitch	1961-1964
Smothers Brothers Comedy Hour	1967-1969
Sonny and Cher Comedy Hour	1971-1974
Steve Allen (Show)	1956-1960
Tennessee Ernie Ford Show	1956-1961
Tonight Show (Jack Paar)	1957-1962

Tonight Show (Steve Allen)	1954-1957
Tonight Show Starring Johnny Carson	1962-1992
Tony Orlando and Dawn	1974-1976
Your Show of Shows	1950-1954

The Daytime Soap Operas

All My Children	1970-2011	41 years
Another World	1964-1999	35 years
As The World Turns	1956-2010	54 years
Dark Shadows	1966-1971	5 years
Days of Our Lives	1965-present	47 years+
The Edge of Night	1956-1984	28 years
General Hospital	1963-present	49 years+
Guiding Light	1952-2009	57 years
Love of Life	1951-1980	29 years
One Life to Live	1968-2012	44 years
Ryan's Hope	1975-1989	14 years
Search for Tomorrow	1951-1986	36 years
The Secret Storm	1954-1974	20 years
The Young and the Restless	1973-present	39 years+

The Mini-Series

I, Claudius	1976
Rich Man, Poor Man	1976
The Godfather: A Novel for Television	1977
Jesus of Nazareth	1977
Roots	1977

Centennial	1978
Holocaust	1978
Tinker Tailor Soldier Spy	1979

Notable Prime Time 1950s-1970s TV Series

(The word "The" has been omitted from the beginning of these TV show titles. This list is not inclusive of all shows, and shows listed may have aired in additional years not listed due to reprisals, variations, re-runs, etc.)

60 Minutes	1968-Present
77 Sunset Strip	1958-1964
Adam-12	1968-1975
Addams Family	1964-1966
Adventures of Jim Bowie	1956-1958
Adventures of Ozzie & Harriet	1952-1966
Adventures of Rin Tin Tin	1954-1959
Adventures of Superman	1952-1958
Alfred Hitchcock Presents/Hour	1955-1965
Alias Smith and Jones	1971-1973
Alice	1976-1985
All In The Family	1971-1979
Amazing Spider-Man	1977-1979
American Bandstand	1952-1989
Andy Griffith Show	1960-1968
Avengers	1961-1969
Baretta	1975-1978
Barnaby Jones	1973-1980

Barney Miller	1975-1982
Bat Masterson	1958-1961
Batman	1966-1968
Battlestar Galactica	1978-1979
Ben Casey	1961-1966
Beverly Hillbillies	1962-1971
Bewitched	1964-1972
Big Valley	1965-1969
Bill Cosby Show	1969-1971
Bing Crosby Show	1964-1965
Bionic Woman	1976-1978
Blue Angels	1960-1961
Bob Cummings Show	1955-1959
Bob Newhart Show	1972-1978
Bonanza	1959-1973
Brady Bunch	1969-1974
Branded	1965-1966
Bridget Loves Bernie	1972-1973
Bronco	1958-1962
Burke's Law	1963-1965
Candid Camera	1948-54, 1960-67
Cannon	1971-1976
Cannonball	1958-1959
Car 54, Where Are You?	1961-1963
CBS Evening News/Walter Cronkite	1962-1981
Charlie's Angels	1976-1981
Checking In	1981

Cheyenne	1955-1963
Chico and the Man	1974-1978
Colt .45	1957-1960
Columbo	1968-1978+
Combat!	1962-1967
Courtship of Eddie's Father	1969-1972
Custer	1967
Daktari	1966-1969
Dallas	1978-1991
Daniel Boone	1964-1970
Davy Crockett	1954-1955
Death Valley Days	1952-1975
December Bride	1954-1959
Defenders	1961-1965
Dennis the Menace	1959-1963
Dick Van Dyke Show	1961-1966
Donna Reed Show	1958-1966
Doris Day Show	1968-1973
Dr. Kildare	1961-1966
Dragnet	1951-59, 1967-70
Dukes of Hazzard	1979-1985
Eight is Enough	1977-1981
Ensign O'Toole	1962-1963
Everglades	1961-1962
F Troop	1965-1967
F.B.I.	1965-1974
Family	1976-1980

Family Affair	1966-1971
Fantasy Island	1978-1984
Father Knows Best	1954-1960
Fish	1977-1978
Flipper	1964-1967
Flo	1980-1981
Flying Nun	1967-1970
Fugitive	1963-1967
Funny Face/Sandy Duncan Show	1971-1972
Fury	1955-1960
Garrison's Gorillas	1967-1968
Gentle Ben	1967-1969
George Burns and Gracie Allen Show	1950-1958
Get Smart	1965-1970
Gidget	1965-1966
Gilligan's Island	1964-1967
Gomer Pyle, U.S.M.C.	1964-1969
Good Heavens	1976
Good Times	1974-1979
Green Acres	1965-1971
Gunsmoke	1955-1975
Happy Days	1974-1984
Harry O	1974-1976
Have Gun, Will Travel	1957-1963
Hawaii Five-O	1968-1980
Hawaiian Eye	1959-1963
Hazel	1961-1966

Here Come The Brides	1968-1970
Here's Lucy	1968-1974
Highway Patrol	1955-1959
Hogan's Heroes	1965-1971
Honey West	1965-1966
Honeymooners	1955-1956
I Dream of Jeannie	1965-1970
I Love Lucy	1951-1957
I Spy	1965-1968
Immortal	1970-1971
Incredible Hulk	1978-1982
Invaders	1967-1968
Ironside	1967-1975
It Takes A Thief	1968-1970
It's About Time	1966-1967
Jeffersons	1975-1985
Julia	1968-1971
Knots Landing	1979-1993
Kojak	1973-1978
Kolchak: The Night Stalker	1974-1975
Kung Fu	1972-1975
Laramie	1959-1963
Lassie	1954-1973
Laverne & Shirley	1976-1983
Lawman	1958-1962
Leave it to Beaver	1957-1963
Lieutenant	1963-1964

Life and Legend of Wyatt Earp	1955-1961
Life and Times of Grizzly Adams	1977-1978
Life of Riley	1953-1958
Little House On The Prairie	1974-1983
Lone Ranger	1949-1957
Loretta Young Show	1953-1961
Lost in Space	1965-1968
Lou Grant	1977-1982
Love Boat	1977-1986
Love, American Style	1969-1974
M*A*S*H	1972-1983
Make Room For Daddy/Danny Thomas	1953-1964
Mama	1949-1957
Man from U.N.C.L.E.	1964-1968
Mannix	1967-1975
Many Loves of Dobie Gillis	1959-1963
Marcus Welby, MD	1969-1976
Mary Hartman, Mary Hartman	1976-1977
Mary Tyler Moore Show	1970-1977
Masterpiece Theatre	1971-Present
Maude	1972-1978
Maverick	1957-1962
Mayberry R.F.D.	1968-1971
McCloud	1970-1977
McHale's Navy	1962-1966
McMillan & Wife	1971-1977
Medical Center	1969-1976

Mickey Mouse Club	1955-1996
Millionaire	1955-1960
Mission Impossible	1966-1973
Mister Ed	1961-1966
Mister Roberts	1965-1966
Mod Squad	1968-1973
Monkees	1966-1968
Mork & Mindy	1978-1982
Movin' On	1974-1976
Munsters	1964-1966
Mutual of Omaha's 'Wild Kingdom'	1963-1988
My Favorite Martian	1963-1966
My Living Doll	1964-1965
My Mother The Car	1965-1966
My Three Sons	1960-1972
Naked City	1958-1963
Night Gallery	1970-1973
No Time For Sergeants	1964-1965
Odd Couple	1970-1975
One Day At A Time	1975-1984
One Step Beyond	1959-1961
Our Miss Brooks	1952-1956
Outer Limits	1963-1965
Partridge Family	1970-1974
Patty Duke Show	1963-1966
People's Choice	1955-1958
Perry Mason	1957-1966

Peter Gunn	1958-1961
Petticoat Junction	1963-1970
Peyton Place	1964-1969
Phil Silvers Show	1955-1959
Phyllis	1975-1977
Playhouse 90	1956-1960
Police Woman	1974-1978
Private Secretary	1953-1957
Rat Patrol	1966-1968
Rawhide	1959-1966
Real McCoys	1957-1963
Rhoda	1974-1978
Rifleman	1958-1963
Rockford Files	1974-1980
Rookies	1972-1976
Room 222	1969-1974
Ropers	1979-1980
Route 66	1960-1964
Roy Rogers	1951-1957
Run For Your Life	1965-1968
S.W.A.T.	1975-1976
Saint	1962-1969
Sanford and Son	1971-1977
Sea Hunt	1958-1961
Six Million Dollar Man	1974-1978
Soap	1977-1981
Soul Train	1971-2006

Star Trek (The Original Series)	1966-1969
Starsky and Hutch	1975-1979
Streets of San Francisco	1972-1977
Sugarfoot	1957-1961
Superman	1964-1966
Surfside 6	1960-1962
Tales of Wells Fargo	1957-1962
Tarzan	1966-1968
Taxi	1978-1983
Texan	1958-1960
That Girl	1966-1971
Then Came Bronson	1969-1970
This Is Your Life	1952-1961
Three's Company	1977-1984
Today Show	1952-Present
Twelve O'Clock High	1964-1967
Twilight Zone	1959-1964
Tycoon	1964-1965
Undersea World of Jacques Cousteau	1968-1975
Untouchables	1959-1963
Virginian	1962-1971
Voyage to the Bottom of the Sea	1964-1968
Wackiest Ship in the Army	1965-1966
Wagon Train	1957-1962
Walt Disney's (Various Titles)	1954-Present
Waltons	1972-1981
Wanted: Dead or Alive	1958-1961

Welcome Back, Kotter	1975-1979
What's Happening!!	1976-1979
White Shadow	1978-1981
Wild, Wild West	1965-1969
WKRP in Cincinnati	1978-1982
Wonder Woman	1975-1979
You Are There	1953-1957
Zorro	1957-1959

Reruns Back In The Day

Do you remember in the 1950s and 1960s watching shows, "shorts" and full length movies from the 1930s-1950s as reruns? We *must* mention what some of us watched every day after school or on Saturdays. Films were presented by different emcees or hosts in various parts of the country, e.g., "Ghoulardi", so there is no nationwide name for the "show" to list here. But typically these classics ran: Charlie Chaplin; The Three Stooges; Laurel and Hardy; Abbot and Costello; Shirley Temple; Judy Garland; Mickey Rooney; Hope and Crosby; Tarzan; Zorro; The Lone Ranger; Roy Rogers; The Little Rascals; Our Gang; Martin and Lewis; Sherlock Holmes; Charlie Chan; Carmen Miranda; Ginger Rogers; Esther Williams; John Wayne and other westerns; Fred Astaire, Gene Kelly and other musicals and dance movies; Vincent Price, Bella Lugosi, Godzilla, Frankenstein, and innumerable mummies, vampires, werewolves, zombies, lagoon and swamp creatures, spacemen, aliens, giant attacking animals and other monster, science fiction and B movie horror films! Pass the milk and graham crackers!

About the Co-Authors

Debbie J. Papay, Attorney

Debbie J. Papay was raised in Elyria, Ohio, before she moved to Toledo to attend Davis College. There she graduated in 1975 with an Associate Degree, summa cum laude. Debbie achieved her B.A. in Business Administration and Management from Siena Heights College, summa cum laude in 1981, and her Doctor of Jurisprudence Degree from the University of Toledo College of Law, magna cum laude in 1985. She began working in law offices in 1974, since 1985 as an attorney concentrating in estate and trust planning, probate, real estate, elder law, Medicaid and the V.A. Pension.

The late baby of a late baby, Debbie was raised with a fondness for "the elders" which has helped shape her practice of law. In 2005 Debbie became the first attorney in northwest Ohio to obtain a Gerontology Certificate from Mercy College. In 2008 she and her law partner, Chris E. Steiner, became the first two area attorneys to be accredited by the Veterans Administration. Since that time Debbie has attended specialized V.A. Pension and Medicaid training in Boston, New Hartford, Chicago, Atlanta, Dallas and Columbus.

While in law school, Debbie's law review article was published and she served as a Note and Comment Editor. Since then Debbie has been a contributing author to two hardbound books: *Strictly Business: Planning Strategies for Privately Owned Businesses*, and *Love, Money, Control: Reinventing Estate Planning*, both Quantum Press, LLC, 2002 and 2004.

Debbie has served on the Boards of Directors of the Lutheran Home at Toledo, Planned Pethood, and Davis College, and been an officer and member of several local professional organizations. Debbie and her husband, Brian Carder, have been married for over 34 years. They make Maumee, Ohio, their home, with Olive, the yellow lab.

Chris E. Steiner, Attorney

Chris E. Steiner attained his Bachelor of Education Degree from the University of Toledo, magna cum laude, in 1974. In 1977, he earned a Doctor of Jurisprudence Degree from its College of Law.

Chris entered the private practice of law in 1978, and became a partner in the law firm of Spengler, Nathanson, Heyman, McCarthy & Durfee in 1984. He worked primarily in the areas of estate planning, business acquisitions and mergers, real estate, and commercial law. After a brief period as a corporate attorney, Chris re-entered the private practice of law in 1986.

Chris concentrates his current practice of law in the areas of estate and life planning, charitable giving, special needs planning, business matters, real estate, and elder law, including the V.A. Pension.

Chris is a contributing author to The *Charitable Giving Handbook*, published by National Underwriter, 1997, and three hardbound books published by Quantum Press: *Giving: Philanthropy for Everyone; Strictly Business: Planning Strategies for Privately Owned Businesses;* and *Love, Money, Control: Reinventing Estate Planning*.

For more than 20 years, Chris has served as the attorney for the Maumee Watershed District, formerly the Toledo District of the United Methodist Church. He is a four time delegate to General and Jurisdictional Conferences from West Ohio.

Chris and his wife, Ann, have four children: two daughters and two sons. They are the proud grandparents of five wonderful grandchildren. Chris is very active in church and community affairs, and also finds time to water ski, umpire high school baseball and softball games, and referee high school and college football games.

BAYER, PAPAY
& STEINER CO., LPA

Attorneys & Counselors at Law

1925 Indian Wood Circle, Suite A
Maumee, Ohio 43537

Debbie J. Papay and Chris E. Steiner are the co-owners of their law firm, Bayer, Papay & Steiner Co., LPA, formed between them in 1998 as a successor to Richard W. Bayer's firm, "Bayer Attorneys." The firm is conveniently located in Maumee's beautiful Arrowhead Park, just off exits from the Ohio Turnpike and Interstates 75 and 475 (US 23), in a one story, accessible building with free, adjacent parking. In keeping with one of their mottos, namely "Educate to Motivate," the attorneys present a free workshop once a month in the law firm's Learning Center on estate planning topics. The attorneys frequently present workshops in outside locations.

Debbie and Chris are both licensed attorneys in the state of Ohio, as well as VA accredited attorneys authorized to prepare, present, and prosecute claims for the Veterans Pension before the Department of Veterans Affairs.

Bayer, Papay & Steiner Co., LPA or its attorneys are members of Wealth Counsel, LLC; NNEPA (National Network of Estate Planning Attorneys LLC); NAELA (National Association of Elder Law Attorneys); the Ohio Forum; the Ohio State, Lucas County and Toledo Bar Associations; Christian Legal Society; and NOGA (Northwest Ohio Gerontological Association). The firm supports the Maumee Chamber of Commerce, as well as a number of other area organizations. Its attorneys attend significant hours of continuing education annually and are in weekly communication with estate planning attorneys around the country on topics benefitting their clients.

Debbie and Chris concentrate their combined law practice in all areas of estate planning and administration and elder law, as well as the areas of law that are closely involved with those activities (for example, real estate and business). They encourage a lifelong relationship with their clients, as well as their next generation. They are mindful of their office mottos, "Plans That Work℠ By People Who Care," and "Helping Seniors and Those Who Love Them."

Debbie and Chris encourage their clients to pass on some personality when they come in to just Will their wallets, and they offer unique tools to do this. Another advantage they have that differentiates Debbie and Chris from many estate planning attorneys is that in *preparing* plans to be implemented in the *future* they have the benefit of knowing "how the story turns out." This means that with over six decades of experience between them administering literally hundreds of decedents' Wills and Trusts, written by them or other attorneys, they have seen how old plans worked (or didn't) when it actually came time to implement them. This experience is invaluable in the planning and drafting stages for new plans. Debbie and Chris also have access to the collective wisdom and experience of nationwide networks of estate planning attorneys to which they belong. For their clients, this is like having a large team of experienced estate planning attorneys in a back office from which to gain additional insight and planning strategies!

Debbie, Chris, Brian Carder, their Operations Director, and their entire team of caring, experienced legal assistants, devote themselves to the thorough and professional service of clients of all ages who want to plan for their future or need to administer the estate or trust of a loved one.

Bayer, Papay & Steiner Co., LPA
By Appointment Only, 419-891-8884
www.PlansThatWork.net
steiner@PlansThatWork.net
papay@PlansThatWork.net